MW00387059

THE SACRED ORIGIN AND NATURE
OF SPORTS AND CULTURE

THE SACRED
ORIGIN AND
NATURE OF
SPORTS
AND CULTURE

GHAZI BIN MUHAMMAD

FONS VITAE

Copyright © 1998 Ghazi bin Mohammad

All rights reserved. No part of this book may be
reproduced or utilized in any form or by any means,
electronic or mechanical, including photocopying and recording
or by any information storage and retrieval system,
without the written permission of the publisher.

Printed in the United States of America

Library of Congress Catalog Card Number: 98–72995

ISBN-1-887752-13-7

Fons Vitae
(Gray Henry, Director)
49 Mockingbird Valley Drive
Louisville, KY 40207-1366
email: Grayh@aol.com
website: www.fonsvitae.com

CONTENTS

ABOUT THE AUTHOR

H.R.H. Prince Ghazi bin Muhammad was educated at Harrow School, received his B.A. at Princeton University *Summa cum laude* and received his Ph.D. from Trinity College, Cambridge University. From 1988–91 he was President of the Jordanian National Basketball Federation and is currently President of the Jordanian National Boxing Foundation. He has published a number of books and articles, and is presently Cultural Secretary to H.M. King Hussein of Jordan. However, the texts contained herein represent strictly his own personal views and opinions.

PUBLISHER'S NOTE: The author's original British spelling, punctuation, and hyphenation have been changed to standard American usage throughout this edition, except for direct quotations.

The reader also will notice that following the mention of the name of a prophet in the text, there is a small seal in Arabic. Around the globe, be it in China or Nigeria, no Muslim would refer to the Prophet Muhammad (ﷺ), to Jesus (عليه السلام) or to any of the other prophets, such as David or Zachariah (عليه السلام), without adding: "May God's peace be upon him, her, or them."

PREFACE

I WROTE THESE two tracts because it seemed to me that there was generally a tremendous amount of confusion about the two subjects, and that perhaps two traditional philosophical monographs of this sort might serve as useful starting points for further reading, if not actually as synopses of that reading itself.

In philosophy, as in horticulture, one "picks cabbages where one finds them," and this is exactly the method I have used here as regards sources and references, not just because *Spiritus ubi vult spirat*, but also because the nature and history of the two subjects considered — particularly sports — were not confined to one civilization, one religion, or one tradition. That is not to say, however, that I personally agree, in every context, with everything written by all my sources, but rather, simply, that I followed the Imam Ali's (ﷺ) advice: "Look at what is said, not at whom is speaking." I pray the reader grant me the same indulgence.

I must thank Rob Baker for all his efforts in "Americanizing" the text and Dr. William Stoddart for his useful suggestions.

Finally, I would also like to thank Dr. Reza Shahkazemi for all his help in proofreading and editing the two texts. I have not always followed all his advice, but I could not have wished for a more astute editor.

GHAZI BIN MUHAMMAD
January 1998

WHAT IS CULTURE?

CULTURE IS "TO KNOW THE BEST
THAT HAS BEEN SAID AND
THOUGHT IN THE WORLD."

MATTHEW ARNOLD, "LITERATURE AND DOGMA"

This essay is divided into the following parts:

(i) INTRODUCTION

SINCE THE TIME of the Renaissance no single word or concept has been more thoroughly discussed or more laboriously examined than the word "culture." It has been called one of the two or three most complicated words in the English language.[1] Admittedly, this is partly because those engaged in such discussions or treatises automatically acquire *ipso facto* a vested interest in elevating the prestige and meaning of the word "culture": evidently the very idea of such discussions or treatises itself pertains to — or falls under — the concept of "culture," and therefore those engaging in them are also in engaging in an assessment of the worth of their own activities. Moreover, some even argue that it is "culture" itself that determines how we define it, and therefore all definitions of it are *a priori* moot: defining it is like the soul trying to define the limits of its own intelligence, and this is obviously impossible since doing so presupposes a greater intelligence that can encompass it.[2] Consequently, the term itself has become a kind of ideological "peg" on which is hung a vague but seemingly endless panoply of ideas and practices whose very diversity and inclusiveness reflect the importance that has been attributed to it. Indeed, everything from civilization itself to shaking hands and nodding, from mythology to cooking, from clothes

1. Raymond Williams, *Keywords* (London: Fonatana, 1983), 87.
2. As Plato says: "The eye cannot see itself." The problem with this argument, however, is that culture is not synonymous with intelligence (which pertains rather to "nature," as will be discussed later) and therefore *is* amenable at least to "functional self-referentiality and definition," just as in language it is functionally possible to refer to and define oneself, or language itself. Moreover, obviously the soul and therefore also culture can, in theological doctrine, be encompassed by "the point of view of" the Spirit or the Uncreated Intellect.

11

fashion to sleeping habits, can now be placed under the category of "culture":

> Culture . . . is one of the most widely used, and abused, words in English. Its meaning blurs and varies according to its context and who is describing it.[3]

However, for all this variety and activity — or perhaps precisely because of it — the term "culture" has retained in the popular consciousness only the basic meaning of "pertaining to the fine arts," and doing so in an entirely artificial, amoral, and even unintelligible way. It is our purpose in what follows to explain and clarify the original and true meaning of the term; to discuss its ideological content and logical implications; and to explore the underlying reality to which it refers,[4] all with the aim of moving some

---

3. *Key Ideas in Human Thought*, ed., Kenneth McLeish (New York: Facts on File, 1993), 178.

4. In sacred and primordial languages (such as classical Arabic and ancient Hebrew) the word *is* mysteriously one with the thing named, because it is exactly a linguistic crystallization (vocal and, when written, visual) of its celestial archetype and essence — hence the theurgic power and magic of sacred formulas, and indeed of all traditional sacred symbols. This is true even for such civilizations as that of the ancient Egyptians:

> Another distinction lacking to ancient Egypt was the one most of us make automatically between the name and the thing [named]. For the ancient Egyptian the name *was* the thing; the real object we separate from its designation was identical with it. (J. M. Roberts, *History of the World* [New York: Oxford University Press, 1993], 88.)

This, however, is evidently not true for modern Western vernacular languages, as Ferdinand de Saussure pointed out at the beginning of this century, for in these languages meaning is (to a certain extent) generated by convention through a tenuous (and shifting, according to the Post-Structuralists) relation between a "signifier" and "signified," and moreover there is always, in linguistic discourse, the problem of *heteroglossia* (to use Bakhtin's term for the "plurality of reality" that escapes language).

way toward restoring both the term and what it refers to their full and proper status. This will be done succinctly in the following way: first, by explaining the original, etymologically derived meaning of the term; second, by reviewing all the concepts and near-synonyms most closely associated with the term, and the differences between it and them, thereby deriving its contemporary meaning and definition; third, by exploring the philosophical content of the term "culture" as it is understood in the modern world; fourth, by considering some of the most important and common uses and associations of the term and by seeing how the "concept" behind it operates in each case; fifth, by discussing the contemporary state of "culture" in the world as a whole; sixth, by speculating on the future of culture, or at least on the main perceptions and views of it; seventh, by showing the power and potential of culture; and eighth — and lastly — by suggesting a moral imperative in and for culture.

(ii) WHAT THE TERM "CULTURE" MEANS DE JURE

To START WITH, let it be said then that the English word "culture" has its origins in the French word *culture*, which in turn comes from the Latin *cultura*. The original meaning of the word — still in usage in English as for example with the term "bacteria culture" or even "agriculture" — is to "till" or "foster," usually applied to crops or land, and in general signifying the "deliberate development of nature." It is obviously related to the term "cultivate" (which in fact has now more or less appropriated the original meaning of *cultura* to itself) as also to the word "cult"[5] through the common idea of devotion, preparation, and servitude. Consequently, the basic definitions of "culture" (in the "human" sense of the term) in *The New Shorter Oxford English Dictionary* run as follows:

> The cultivation or development of the mind, manners, etc.; improvement by education and training. (B) Refinement of mind, tastes, and manners; artistic and individual development; the artistic and intellectual side of civilization. (C) A particular form, stage, or type of intellectual development or civilization in a society; a society or group characterized by its distinctive customs, achievements, products, outlook, etc. (D) The distinctive customs, achievements, product, outlook, etc. of a society or group; the way of life of a society or group.

5. Strictly speaking the word "cult" comes from the Latin *cultus* meaning "to worship," but evidently the word *cultus* itself is etymologically connected to *cultura*.

14

It will be noted the four definitions given above are merely the individual general; individual refined; collective general; and collective refined — permutations respectively of one and the same idea. Similarly, the etymology of the Arabic word for "culture" — *thaqafah* — also comprises the same basic themes of experience, intelligence, moral rectitude, training, education and nurture:

> *Thaqafa* (v.) (I)[6] to find, meet (someone); *thaqifah* and *thaqufah* to be skilful, smart, clever. (II) To make straight, straighten (something); to correct, set right, straighten out (s.th.); to train, form, teach, educate etc. . . . *Thaqafah* (n.) culture, refinement; education, (pl.-*at*) culture, civilization. *Tathqif* cultivation of the mind; training, education; instruction.[7]

It is evident, however, that dictionary definitions and etymological evidence, while adequate in themselves to conveying the original, basic, *de jure* sense of the term "culture," do not clarify and specify all its *de facto* implications and connotations.

---

6. Every word in Arabic can be reduced to a basic tri-literal root (except in the case of onomatopoeic words which can be reduced to quadri-literal) — in this case "*th-q-f*" — from which ten main different "verbal forms" can be produced. The first "verbal form" (I) indicates the simplest and most basic verbal meaning; the second form (II) intensifies the basic verbal meaning; the third form (III) adds the idea of additional "activity" to the basic verbal meaning, and so on.

7. *The Hans Wehr Dictionary of Modern Written Arabic*, ed. J. M. Cowan (Ithaca, N.Y.: Cornell University Press, 1961), 104.

(iii) WHAT THE TERM "CULTURE" MEANS DE FACTO

To UNDERSTAND THE implications and connotations of the word "culture," then, we have to review some common collocations of the term and highlight the differences between it and them. First, then, let it be said that while the concept of culture includes — and is inextricably bound up with — education, the two are not synonymous: the word "education" is usually taken to refer to the formal instruction of academic disciplines and mental and linguistic skills, and to the process of learning and retaining information by youth and young adults (albeit that education can continue at any age).[8] "Culture," on the other hand refers not so much to particular formal ideas — although evidently it is not unrelated to these — as to the imprints and influence of these ideas on both the individual and collective consciousnesses. Thus, culture is not so much the aggregate of knowledge or information — or even ideas — of a given set of people or of a society, but rather the conscious and subconscious notional matrix through which the world is known and perceived, and from which issue social customs and modes of thought and behavior. The concept

8. The word "education" is defined in *The Concise Oxford Dictionary* as "systematic instruction" and "development of character or mental powers." In *The New Shorter Oxford English Dictionary* it is defined as: (1) The process of nourishing or rearing. (2) The process of bringing up children in particular manners, habits, or ways of life. (3) The systematic instruction, schooling, or training of children and young people, or, by extension, instruction obtained in adult life; the whole course of such instruction received by a person. Also, provision of this as an aspect of public policy. (4) The development of mental or physical powers; molding of character.

of "culture" is therefore broader and looser than that of "education," since it is concerned with the whole of society and, indeed, human activity, and not just formal instruction in certain accepted disciplines of knowledge.

Another term with which the idea of culture is often linked and sometimes confused is the term "heritage." In the sense in which we mean the term it is defined (in *The Concise Oxford Dictionary*) as "inherited circumstances, benefits" and "a nation's historic buildings, monuments, countryside, etc., esp. when regarded as worthy of preservation." Thus obviously the concept of "heritage" is one that refers to things "concrete" and "definite" (whereas that of "culture" can either be "concrete" or "abstract"), and one that relates exclusively to the past. Needless to say, of course, "culture" also relates inextricably to the past — how could it be otherwise? The future has not yet come to pass, and the present is but an intangible, if not ineffable, moment which is constantly and instantaneously flowing from and into the past — but "heritage" does so in a way that is "static" and "fixed" and no longer vital.

The term "tradition" (from the Latin *traditio* meaning to "hand over" or "deliver" and generally indicating a custom[9] or belief handed down in a non-written form over a number of generations), like the term "heritage," inherently contains the idea of the past, with the following differences: unlike "heritage," "tradition" is not usually "concrete" or "physical" (except occasionally, in an extrinsic way, by association with particular locations or

---

9. The term "custom" (from the Latin *consuetudo* via the Old French *coustume*) itself means, "a social habit," or according to *The New Shorter Oxford English Dictionary*: "A habitual or usual practice; a common way of behaving." It is often associated with the idea of culture, but unlike the terms mentioned above it is not usually confused with it, because it is known to be a constituent part of it, and not a synonym for it.

17

objects); unlike "heritage," "tradition" implies something handed down deliberately and through human means; and unlike "heritage" the term "tradition" has religious undertones, not only because there are known religious traditions in Judaism, Christianity, and Islam, but also because it could be argued that everything truly "traditional" has its origin in primordial religion and mythology.[10] Thus "tradition" also differs from culture by being related more holistically to the past, by generally being "abstract," by necessarily having religious connotations ("culture" does not always, as will shortly be discussed) and by being handed down deliberately through human transmission. One might even say that there is a kind of "holy monotony" about "tradition" which contrasts with the "worldly dynamism" of "culture."

The term "civilization" — from the Latin words *civitas* meaning "city" and *civilis* meaning "citizen," and defined as an "advanced stage or system of social development" or "peoples of the world that are regarded as having this"[11] — is one that also generally refers to the past, or at least to the present from a historical perspective. Furthermore, as with the term "heritage," it also differs from the idea of "culture" by being more "concrete" and "definite." Unlike "heritage," however, it is restricted by definition to *urban* culture, society, and history. It therefore implies moral prejudice in favor of the Darwinian notions of social "progress," despite the utilitarian undercurrents endemic to these notions; despite the intrinsic spiritual and moral quality of many nomadic and "hunter–gatherer" societies (going back at least 30,000 years — when the first mature and stylized cave art appears — and up to

10. For example, it is said that the Western tradition of touching wood for luck is a reminder of the Ark which saved Noah and his family from the flood. However, this line of argument obviously depends on what is considered truly "traditional" in the first place.

11. See *The Concise Oxford Dictionary*.

the present day, in certain parts of the world); and despite all the beauty, wisdom, and genius of many oral cultures.

Four other concepts are also commonly associated with that of "culture": the humanities, the fine arts, language, and religion. The humanities are quite simply a subset — albeit an academic one — of culture consisting of the Classics (Greek and Latin), literature, and philosophy. The remaining three concepts, however, are ones which "overlap" with the term "culture," even if they are not as often confused or intertwined with it as the four terms discussed earlier (education, heritage, tradition, and civilization). Taking them in order, the first thing to be said is that the word "culture" is nowadays often popularly reduced to the sum total of the "fine" and "performing" arts[12] or to "high culture" in general. Now obviously the arts form a large and very important part of culture, because they are (in principle, at least) the ultimate repository of the human urge to create and, in particular, to create beauty[13]; because they are the second greatest source of sensible beauty[14] in the world — after

---

12. The "fine arts" are defined, in *The Concise Oxford Dictionary*, as "Poetry, music, and the visual arts, esp. painting, sculpture, and architecture." We prefer to divide the arts into four categories — physical, mental, visual, and auditory — according to what kind of beauty they produce: "physical" would include architecture, dancing, sculpture (in the West) and handicrafts etc.; "mental" would include poetry, literature, *belles lettres*, and the like; "visual" would obviously refer to the visual arts: painting, calligraphy, and so on; and "auditory" would evidently be the realm of music. If we include the "performing arts" in these then evidently they would also comprise theatre, dance, and nowadays, presumably, cinema.

13. The urgency and importance of the human need to create and to create beauty, in particular, should not be underestimated. The Prophet Muhammad (ﷺ) said: *God created Adam in His own image* (*Musnad Ibn Hanbal*, I: 251 and *Sahih Muslim*, XLV: 32). Similarly, the Book of Genesis (1: 27) records that: *God created man in His own image.* Now to be made in the image of the Creator is as much as anything to be a creator of sorts oneself, to be *homo fabiens*. . . .

14. There are many kinds of beauty that are not sensible: as mentioned above there is poetry and other kinds of "mental" beauty, and there is of course

natural beauty (which includes, of course, human beauty) — and finally because the forms they generate and produce constitute one of the most important and yet least controversial of all modes[15] of

---

virtue, which is the beauty of soul or "inner beauty," and which undeniably reveals itself in noble actions for *Ye shall know them by their fruits* (Matthew 7:16).

And this of course does not even take into consideration spiritual and, ultimately, Divine beauty. Plotinus says:

> Beauty addresses itself chiefly to sight; but there is a beauty for the hearing too, as in certain combinations of words and in all kinds of music, for melodies and cadences are beautiful; and minds that lift themselves above the realm of sense to a higher order are aware of beauty in the conduct of life, in actions, in character, in the pursuits of the intellect; and there is the beauty of the virtues. What loftier beauty there may be, yet, our argument will bring to light [i.e. spiritual and Divine beauty]. (Plotinus, *The Enneads*, I. VI. I., 45)

It goes without saying, moreover, that beauty in itself is essential to our lives not only because of the joy, peace. and message of truth it affords, but because it, together with goodness — which as we have just said is merely inner beauty — suffices to produce love, our most basic emotional need, in whoever beholds and recognizes it:

> "Now, remember, in addition to these points, what you said in your speech about what it is that Love loves. If you like, I'll remind you. I think you said something like this: . . . quarrels were settled by love of beautiful things, for there is no love of ugly ones [in respect of their ugliness as such]. Didn't you say something like that?"
> "I did," . . . said Agathon.
> "And that's a suitable thing to say, my friend," said Socrates. . . . "Now take it a little further. Don't you think that good things are always beautiful as well?" (Plato, *The Symposium of Love*, 201A–201C, trans. Nehamas and Woodruff [Indianapolis: Hacket, 1989], 43.)

15. A case in point par excellence of this is Islamic calligraphy and architecture, the two main branches of Islamic art: in the modern western world, Islam is everywhere, for various reasons, vilified and misunderstood, and yet Islamic art — from the *Taj Mahal* to the Great Mosque at Cordoba — is everywhere admired and studied. Art can thus effectively impart to great numbers of people the wisdom, beauty, and ideas of a civilization across the barriers of time, place, and, dare it be said, ignorance and prejudice.

communication, instruction, and edification in the world. However, for all that, "culture" is definitely not limited to the arts, as is revealed by any elementary consideration of the existence of different social customs or *moeurs* of societies without fine arts as such, these customs being undeniably a part of culture.[16]

The case of "language" is somewhat different, for no one would normally replace or even confuse it with the concept of "culture," or *vice versa*. Nevertheless, there are, on the one hand, certain modern literary critics and philosophers who argue that language determines, or at least limits and shapes, thought and hence also culture; and on the other hand those modern anthropologists who argue that it is culture that determines, or at least frames and defines, language. Furthermore, it is occasionally also argued that culture is a language that can be deciphered according to the internal logic, rules, structures, and patterns of languages, and that conversely language is a culture, since the natural syntax of each language is not inherently "culture-free" but actually predisposes the practitioners of that language toward certain thoughts, certain ideas, certain concepts, and ultimately, a certain culture. Now obviously both arguments are extreme and polarized, and both are susceptible to logical and dialectical *deconstruction*; indeed, one need only consider physical gestures or other non-verbal forms of communication to see that the truth of the matter must lie somewhere between the two positions. Also, one can easily point to historical examples where the language of a nation or society has been changed without the culture being fundamentally altered. For example, the official and written language of Egypt after Alexander became Greek without

16. Although in general it is true that the "fine arts" are but a subset of "culture," it nevertheless must be said that if "sacred art" is part of the "fine arts" then there exists a part of the arts which goes beyond culture: the spiritual content of sacred art obviously transcends "culture" as such, and both its origin and final end are not terrestrial but Heavenly.

the culture significantly changing until the advent of Christianity. Similarly, one can easily point to examples of radical cultural changes that have not fundamentally altered the language of a nation or society. For example, the Arabic language did not significantly change in the Arab world for over a thousand years, from the time of the Arab *Jahiliyyah*, before the Prophet Muhammad (ﷺ), in the sixth century A.D. until the crystallization of modern standard Arabic in the last two hundred years; and this, despite the advent of a new world civilization, and despite countless contacts, invasions, incursions, and conquests by countless nations from Mongols to Turks to Europeans to Africans to Persians, and despite the eclipse of the nomadic lifestyle by a sedentary or farming one. Thus, it would be more accurate to say that language and culture profoundly influence each other, to the point where the presence of the one invariably means the presence of the other. At most, one could perhaps venture to say that culture creates things out of concepts and tendencies already latent in language, and that language prefigures the possibilities that culture brings forth from it (the numinous ineffability of spiritual art notwithstanding).

The case of "religion" is again different. It could not be said that there is a kind of "symbiosis" between religion and culture, as for example between religion and language. Rather, it could be said that religion is "greater" than culture: it is greater in the sense that although religions act largely on the earthly plane, their focus is the plane of Heaven — *religio* meaning, in Latin, "to bind" man to God — unlike culture, which in itself is evidently mostly an earthly affair. It is also greater in the sense that religion largely creates and determines the cultures of civilizations and societies (or did, until the Renaissance and the dawn of the secular modern age). That is to say that religions deal primarily with spiritual principles, with Heaven, with the Hereafter and with the Divine Reality, all of which transcend culture as such, which is limited to the realm of "human" facts, this world, its phenomena and life in it. Similarly, Revelations and / or new religions — and these by definition are not themselves "culturally determined" since they issue from Heaven — usually bear within themselves the seeds of a future millennial civilization's entire culture and sensibility (and thereby generate and determine these) including its laws, its values, its customs, its future traditions, its educational systems, its socio-economic structure, its arts, its food, its clothing, its architecture, and indeed most every other sphere of human activity. This dominance of religion over culture is easy to show in the case of a civilization like that of the Islamic world or of Judaism in the diaspora, where the origin and formative period of the religion are fairly well documented and where their sacred laws clearly regulate and pervade every aspect life from birth to death. However, it is perhaps not so easy to show this (although it is no less true) in the case of those religions whose historical roots are more nebulous or others, like Christianity, which have common law instead of — or rather in the absence of — sacred law.

On the other hand, it must also be said that there are two aspects of culture that are not strictly speaking determined by religion, nor even altered by it, either because religions commend them (or are silent about them, thereby *de facto* tolerating them), or because they are natural phenomena that religions cannot — and do not even want to — change. The first category includes such basically social phenomena as ethnic customs; historical experience (which it is impossible to forget); technological inventions (which it is next to impossible to un-invent, although Japan apparently un-invented the cannon, for ethical reasons during the Tokugawa Shoganate from the beginning of the seventeenth century until the middle of the nineteenth); and perhaps language (which a religion either enshrines — if its Revelation or sacred texts are in that language — or merely adapts to, since it is forced to use it to communicate, even if it

23

"fixes" it in the process).[17] The second category includes such basically natural phenomena as the environment (which necessarily influences culture in a myriad of ways: from how to cope with weather conditions and climate, to agriculture to the psychological impact of the natural background), racial identity, and genius (which obviously influence the mentality of a nation or people *a priori*). Nevertheless, even if religion does not determine these two categories of phenomena, it could be said that on the one hand it suffuses society with the imprint of the spirit, and on the other hand it heightens man's awareness of the imprint of the spirit already infused in nature.

Finally, it must also be said that there is evidently such a thing as secular culture, usually after the decline of a religious civilization as in the case of Rome or as with the modern West. Although in many ways it usually retains the memory — and thus the influence — of the religious culture preceding it, nevertheless when secular culture arises, it can potentially be integrally and intrinsically atheistic. For example, the same land, race, and civilization which produced the Venerable Bede's *Ecclesiastical History of the English People* has produced, in our day, "tabloid journalism," each being part of a real "culture," without the one having anything truly in common with the other. This shows that religion (in this case Christianity) can create and determine a "culture," but that culture can, and sometimes does, exist without religion.

Having thus considered the etymological origin of the word "culture" and hence its *de jure* meaning, and having thus considered its many near-synonyms and those concepts most closely associated

17. The Qur'an, in Islam, is an example *par excellence* of religion enshrining a (sacred) language — and enshrine is the proper word since the content of the Qur'an is Uncreated — and the King James Bible, in Protestant Christianity, is an example of a religion "fixing" a language for several centuries, and indeed that particular translation remains to this day (along with Shakespeare and the Oxford English Dictionary) the reference and standard for proper English.

with it (and the differences between it and them), it is perhaps at this stage worthwhile venturing to adumbrate our own *de facto* definition of the term. Before doing so, however, it might be helpful to briefly recapitulate the following points: culture is both broader and less formal than education, and whereas education consists of teaching people certain ideas, culture consists of the ideas people actually have. Similarly, culture is less "concrete" than heritage, but more ongoing and more "vital." Culture is equally less "concrete" than civilization, but it is not, as a concept, limited to a historical perspective like civilization, nor indeed to the activity of urban society. Then, culture in general includes the arts but is not limited to them (although there is a dimension of sacred art that transcends "culture"). Conversely, religion in general includes culture, but is not limited to it — and there is a part of culture that, strictly speaking, lies outside religion. Finally, culture and language mutually influence each other — but are not synonymous — and it could be said that language is a kind of culture, and culture a kind of language. Putting all these ideas together with the etymological definition of the word as stated at the onset, we arrive at the following statement[18]:

> "Culture" can generally be said to be the "essential stuff" — the intellectual, moral, social, and historical content and fabric — of human societies and civilizations. It includes not only their fine and performing arts but also *a fortiori* their customs, habits, forms, features, styles, experiences, unspoken ideas and attitudes — in short, the living, on-going underlying content of everything in the world that is man-made and not natural or spiritual (in the proper, transcendent sense of the term).

18. Our definition can obviously be *deconstructed*. Nevertheless it maintains a certain operative usefulness and meaning of the kind that gives existence to such things as dictionaries.

(iv) WHAT THE TERM "CULTURE" IMPLIES

THE PHILOSOPHICAL AND ideological content[19] and implications contained "within" the term "culture" can also now be surmised from everything already discussed. Basically, it can be said that "culture" implies the whole process of the nurture of nature with a view to its betterment. More specifically, it can be said that the idea of "culture" includes the sum total of what falls under the category of "nurture" in the great contemporary debate about whether it is "nature" or "nurture" that determines human behavior: since "culture" potentially includes everything that is manmade, and everything that makes human civilization, society, interaction, and ambience different from the society and interaction of higher animals (even in light of what we now know about the complexity of the latter), it is considered to be half responsible

19. Although there have been many excellent and famous treatises that have discussed the content of the term "culture," its ramifications, the concept behind it, the changes in what the term has come to mean, and the changes in "culture" itself , standard reading on these issues must start with *Notes towards the Definition of Culture* by T. S. Eliot (London: Faber and Faber, 1948) and *In Bluebeard's Castle: Notes towards the Redefinition of Culture* by George Steiner (New Haven: Yale University Press, 1971). Other essential writings about culture in general and "high culture" in particular include: Matthew Arnold's *Culture and Anarchy* (London: Smith, Elder, and Co., 1869); his "Literature and Dogma" (1873); *Culture: A Critical Review of Concepts and Definitions* (Cambridge, Mass.: Papers of the Peabody Museum, 1952); Raymond Williams, *Culture and Society* (New York: Harper and Row, 1958); E. D. Hirsch, *Cultural Literacy* (Boston: Houghton Mifflin, 1987); E. D. Hirsch et al., *The Dictionary of Cultural Literacy*, 2d ed. (Boston: Houghton Mifflin, 1993); and perhaps Harold Bloom's, *The Western Canon* (New York: Harcourt Brace, 1994).

— genetics and nature being the other half — for all human behavior.

Now all this has a number of further logical implications that are themselves also inextricably linked, as undertones, to the idea of "culture." Specifically, the aforementioned debate about "nature vs. nurture," whether it be centred in the modern fields of psychology, anthropology, sociology, biochemistry, biology, chemistry or even physics, ignores the existence of free will as a central component in human behavior, alongside both natural disposition and environmental influences. That is to say that not only does this debate suggest that human behavior is determined — rather than just very much affected — by psychological, anthropological, sociological, biochemical etc. givens and influences, but it also suggests that man has no free will and therefore is nothing but a socio-biochemical automaton. In fact, it further denies the very existence of man as he is traditionally defined, and even denies the existence of God, not only because lack of human free will implies this precisely, but also because the debate also excludes predestiny. Now it must be said that the idea of the coexistence of free will and predestiny is a conundrum and a dialectic — although, of course, many throughout the history of religion have explained this dialectic — just as it must be said that even traditional religious psychology admits that after an excess of either good or bad the soul becomes more and more "bound" by its own actions. However, this is still not the same as denying free will altogether and having a secular perspective, and these are precisely the philosophical underpinnings that the "nature vs. nurture" debate lends to the term "culture."

These "secular implications" will doubtless come as no surprise, bearing in mind the differences between religion and culture as discussed in the previous section. It remains only to be said that the first two meanings of the term "culture" quoted at the onset of the essay from *The New Shorter Oxford English Dictionary* ("A" and "B":

"cultivating of the mind" and "intellectual training and refinement") date back, according to *The Concise Oxford Dictionary of English Etymology*, to the sixteenth and nineteenth centuries respectively.[20] In other words, they date back to the times when secularism had begun to become contemplated again, and then actually become real again (respectively) for the first time, in many European states, since the end of the (pagan) Roman Empire. Moreover, the second, latter meaning is nothing other than a more rarified and humanistic — and hence secular — version of the first. We may thus conclude that the secular connotations of the word "culture," are, in the West at least, becoming progressively stronger with the passage of time, and, as will later be seen, with the increasing atheism of Western society.

20. *The Concise Oxford Dictionary of English Etymology*, ed. T. F. Hoad, 108.

(v) HOW THE TERM "CULTURE"
IS USED

TURNING NOW TO some of the most important and common uses and associations of the term "culture" — outside of its mainstream meanings as discussed above — with a view to understanding how the concept of "culture" operates in each case, it must first be said that in our day almost every scientific, academic, professional or communal vocation, discipline, or field of specialization uses the term "culture" in association with its own sphere of interest. For example, one hears of "legal culture," "military culture," "academic culture," "church" or "mosque culture," "computer culture," "television culture," "political culture," "democratic culture," "nationalist culture," "scientific culture," "materialist culture," "popular culture," "street culture"; and even of a special culture among archeologists, writers, historians, mathematicians, physicists, doctors, journalists, students, and so on. One even hears of "honor among thieves" and "codes" of behavior and dress among modern "street gangs." It is in fact doubly appropriate to use the term "culture" under such circumstances because all these "fields of life" involve particular and man-made circumstances, and because they all invariably involve some kind of special education (albeit often informal and "applied") knowledge, experience, or initiation. Now, while the term "culture" itself takes on different shades of connotation and implication every time it is used in conjunction with a different term, it nevertheless provides a kind of ideological "umbrella" for all these different activities and ambiences. In other words, although the term "culture" adapts ever so slightly to different contexts, it

29

nevertheless operates as a kind of generic container for the contents of different "fields of experience."

All of this has three subtle effects: it renders intelligible "fields of particular activity and experience" by lending them "being" through having their own collective nomenclature (namely, the word "culture"); it crystallizes the distinctiveness of each of these particular "fields" or "areas" by lending them "authenticity" through having their own individual nomenclatures (i.e., "legal," "military," "academic" etc. culture); and it links the different "fields of particular activity and experience" together by having their own common yet differing nomenclature (i.e., "legal culture," "military culture," "academic culture"). In short, the word "culture" used in conjunction with other designations gives form and meaning to the sum total of everything associated with these designations.

Much the same can be said about all the modern derivatives of the term "culture": "culture shock," "subculture," "high culture," "cultured," "uncultured," and so on: not only do these terms refer to man-made things, they are also in part created — through delimitation — by the terms themselves. Hence a "culture-shock" is not just a jarring change of social context that one undergoes passively, but a phenomenon of change that is all the more perturbing because one knows the word and knows that one is supposed to be perturbed. Similarly, a "subculture" is all the more esoteric and clandestine — as well as more recognizable — because there is a word for it, because it contains the term "culture" and because most people are familiar with it. Of course, it could be said that all words in a certain sense create their own meanings — and, indeed, it is not our purpose to broach the complexities of linguistic theory and literary criticism here — but nevertheless most nouns and verbs refer to real things and actions which exist prior to any linguistic recognition of them. This is not the same as with the word "culture" and with all those terms associated with it or used in conjunction with it, not merely because it refers to something man-made, but also because it refers to an ideology which is nowadays at the heart of understanding how language and meaning is communicated in the first place.

(vi) THE REALITY OF CULTURE AS IT IS TODAY

TURNING NOW TO the reality of culture in the modern world, it will immediately be obvious that the same six or seven main world cultural traditions — stemming from the world's major religions (Jewish, Christian, Islamic, Hindu, Buddhist, Taoist–Confucian, Shamanist / Animist)[21] — that existed five hundred or a thousand years ago, still survive today and, to a certain extent, shape our world, ethnic diversity notwithstanding, as "basic cultural blocs." However, it will also immediately be obvious that radical and profound change has affected every one of these "civilizations" — and, in fact, all of them together — creating everywhere an unprecedented state of disequilibrium and upheaval which we now simply collectively know as the "culture of the modern world." This "disequilibrium and upheaval" has four undeniable major causes:

The first, clearly, is that never in the history of the world has there been such a plethora of technology and machinery cluttering the lives of ordinary people, especially in developed nations and among urban populations: the world has seen more technological change in the last 200 years than in the last 6000 years of High Civilization,[22] and the life of the average person has been altered

---

21. By Shamanism we mean both Hyperborean Shamanism and the Native American religions — North and South — and by Animism we mean both African and Aboriginal Australian, if these two may indeed be linked by one word.

22. There are even certain years in the twentieth century which have witnessed as much technological and qualitative change as Pharaonic Ancient Egypt did in its whole 3500 years of High Civilization!

beyond recognition, through motor engines and through electricity; through telephones and televisions; through airplanes and through the demographic explosion; through the fear of atomic/nuclear weapons and through computers; through modern "high-technology" and super-conductors, and so on. It would be impossible to document all the individual changes in the daily lives of human beings brought about over the last couple of centuries, so it must suffice to say that all these changes have had an indelible and irreversible impact on both the nature of human souls and the nature of the world they inhabit and thereby also on both the subjective and objective dimensions of culture.

The second cause of cultural "disequilibrium and upheaval," equally clearly, is that never before has there been so much secularism — and even downright atheism — in the world: although it is true that the world before the Renaissance had seen this phenomenon before, it only ever occurred briefly during the decadent final phase of a civilization or empire — such as the Roman — which had in itself originally been deeply religious and devotional. Can one begin to compare, for example, the Rome which resisted Hannibal at the end of the third century B.C., and which, as evinced in Livy, spent more of its time praying, fasting and sacrificing for deliverance (whatever one thinks of their theology and religion) than it did fighting and preparing for war, to the moribund Rome of 410 A.D. or even of the Emperor Caligula in the first century A.D.? However, although there have been periods over history of relative religious decline, these have always been limited both in extent and in time, and never before has there existed entire nations where the majority of people do not believe in the Divine and where the central focus of culture is not religious. As J. M. Roberts says:

> It is an immensely complicated problem to distinguish
> how modern civilization, the first, so far as we know,

which does not have some formal structure of religious belief at its heart, came into being. Perhaps we cannot separate the role of the city in breaking down religious observance from, say, that of science and philosophy in corrupting the belief of the educated. Yet a new future was visible already in the European industrial population of 1870, much of it literate, alienated from traditional authority, secular-minded and beginning to be conscious of itself as an entity. This was a different basis for civilization from anything yet seen.[23]

Moreover, the demise of religion has meant, all over the world, a descent into the "commercial," "popular" and generally "low" culture with which we are all now so familiar: the world of "junk food," blue jeans, "pop" music, prime-time television, modern art, vulgar language, and sexual permissiveness. Religion had stood against these things (notwithstanding the doomed attempts of certain denominations to "compromise with the modern world"), and to a certain extent held them in check, insisting on man's theomorphic nature, and thus his celestial dignity, or rather, potential dignity. However, with the rise of "secular culture," the lowest and most facile elements in the collective human consciousness, from which these things issue, were bound to arise, and indeed now look poised not just to sweep away the remnants of "religious culture" but also all living "high culture" as well. By "religious culture" we mean the specifically sacred customs and art stemming directly from a religion — such as traditional mosque architecture or Christian icon-making for example — and by "high culture" we mean, for example, Aristotle,[24] Ibn Khaldun, Shakespeare and Mozart: culture that,

23. J. M. Roberts, *History of the World*, 688.
24. Essentially the whole of philosophy, it has been said many times, is contained in the writings of Plato and Aristotle, but we say Aristotle here and not

while not sacerdotal, is nevertheless fully consonant *de jure* with religious principles, and which in fact can be viewed, more or less as the case may be, as their "earthly" or "horizontal" refractions. However, if the decline of "religious culture" is only too obvious, the plight of "high culture" needs some clarifying:

> We have seen something of the collapse of hierarchies and of the radical changes in the value-systems [of high culture] which relate personal creation with death. These mutations have bought an end to classical literacy. By that I mean something perfectly concrete. The major part of western literature, which has been for two thousand years and more so deliberately interactive, the work echoing, mirroring, alluding to, previous works in the tradition, is now quickly passing out of reach. Like far galaxies bending over the horizon of invisibility, the bulk of English poetry, from Caxton's Ovid to *Sweeney among the Nightingales*, is now modulating from active presence into the inertness of scholarly conservation. Based, as it firmly is, on a deep, many-branched anatomy of classical and scriptural reference, expressed in a syntax and vocabulary of heightened tenor, the unbroken arc of English poetry, of reciprocal discourse that relates

Plato, for, as anyone who knows the *Phaedrus*, the *Phaedo* or the *Seventh Letter* will concur, Plato, like Plotinus, is, despite his casual language, his apparently unsystematic way of discussing issues, and his logical method of didactic questioning (now eponymously known as "Socratic questioning," Socrates being the interlocutor in question in these dialogues) a *religious*, if not a *mystic*, writer, whatever one may think of his (Pythagorean) religion. In fact, it should be pointed out that while much of "high culture" in the West is Classical (Ancient Greek and Latin) in origin, not all Classical culture is "high" (some is religious, and some, indeed, is "low," witness Sophism, Epicureanism, and Scepticism); equally, not all "high culture" in the West is of Classical origin, as precisely is shown by the examples of Mozart and Shakespeare.

Chaucer and Spenser to Tennyson and to Eliot, is fading rapidly from the reach of natural reading. . . .

American libraries, universities, archives, museums, cen-tres for advanced study, are now the indispensable record and treasure-house of civilization. It is here that the European artist and scholar must come to see the cherished after-glow of his culture. Though often obsessed with the future, the United States is now, certainly in regard to the humanities, the active watchman of the classical past.[25]

The third cause of cultural "disequilibrium and upheaval" is to a certain extent a product of, and reaction to the second cause (the rise of secularism) although at first sight the two might seem dia-metrically opposed: it is the rise of religious fundamentalism,[26] all over the world, and in all the world's major religions. The rise of secularism has paradoxically contributed by way of militant and ignorant reaction, to the rise of fundamentalism. For the banners of fundamentalism invariably contain slogans against atheism and secularism, and draw many simple believers to them on that account. Now it may well be asked how is this leading to "disequi-librium and upheaval" among traditional religious culture, if secu-larism only leads to "more religion"? The answer is that the reli-gious fundamentalism which is waxing in the modern world is vast-ly and qualitatively different from the traditional religion which is

25. George Steiner, A Reader (New York: Oxford University Press, 1984), 423, 429.

26. Actually, the term "fundamentalism," as applied to iconoclastic and politically militant religion (either in "doctrine" or "practice") is a misnomer, because all authentic religions are "fundamentalist" in that they pertain to the fundamentals of life and of existence, and in that they demand both the body and soul of man. Nevertheless, the current meaning of the term is clear, as are its connotations, especially of aggressive political activism.

waning, and that the difference between them is, precisely, that fundamentalism is opposed to all traditional "religious culture" as such (and therefore, in the end, bound to damage and impoverish religion as such). Specifically, the phenomenon of fundamentalism is typically characterized by the following six features: it is iconoclastic and cares nothing for the concept of sacred art (and therefore winds up *de facto* accepting "profane" or "secular" art)[27]; it takes the Scriptures literally and without metaphor and *a fortiori* without esoteric exegesis or the "Sciences of the Book" (but does not for all that bother to explain the hermeneutical sciences or how "meaning" is conveyed in language anyway); it reduces virtue — a state of soul — to following a set of rules (as if the rules were not there to teach virtue in the first place rather than *vice versa*, and as if it were not the case that, as St. Bernard of Clairvaux put it, "the road of bitterness leads to hell"); it simplifies doctrine, theology, metaphysics, ontology, philosophy, soteriology, cosmology, mysticism, and in fact all sciences related to the Attributes of God, Spirit, or the soul to a bare, often unpalatable, minimum; it indulges itself in a kind of "feel-good" parochialism whereby everyone who follows their specific ideas is "good" and headed for salvation, and everyone else is surely damned (as if this judgment were

---

27. Two examples should serve amply to illustrate this point: the same Evangelical Christian fundamentalists who reject the habits of monks and who reject the Latin Mass wear modern suits and preach on television. Equally, the same Islamic fundamentalists who reject the idea of a *minbar* (a wooden flight of stairs — usually intricately worked — with a seat atop them upon which the sheikh sits during the Friday sermon in the mosque while he is preaching), under the pretext that the Prophet (ﷺ) used only to sit on a tree trunk, wind up bringing a Western lounge chair into the mosque and sitting on it! And this despite the fact that for over a thousand years the most pious Muslims in history have sat on these in the greatest and most beautiful mosques in the world; that the style and idea of these *minbar*s are inherently consonant with everything in Islam, and in particular, with the Friday prayer; and that the traditional Arab and Muslim practice is to sit on the ground, and not on a chair.

not God alone's to make and as if the celestial religions did not all teach as much); and, finally, it throws the full force of its weight into political activism, in an almost nationalistic way, seeking to empower itself politically, either through democratic means, or as a last resort (although successful instances of this are still relatively rare) through revolution (as if the primary focus of religion were to conquer the world for the world's sake, rather than to guide people to faith, good works, and salvation).

This is a blight that has afflicted more or less all the world's traditional populous religions: Judaism, Christianity, Islam, and even, recently, Hinduism — as evinced by Bharata Janatra Party (B.J.P.) for example — and Buddhism (as seen in Burma, for instance). However, the details of one concrete example — the case of Islam — should suffice to show precisely how traditional religious culture in general is being corroded by fundamentalism. In Islam, the fundamentalists variously reject all notions of sacred art, "golden proportions" (in geometry), integral harmony, beauty of aspect, nobility of material, or perfection of composition, and this even in architecture and calligraphy, the "sacred arts" *par excellence* of Islam because they house prayer and the Word of God respectively. Equally, they say that non-legislative verses[28] in the Qur'an should be accepted "without explanation" (*bila kayf*); they reject the notion that it contains "metaphor" (*majaz*, a concept which in Arabic includes metonymy, synecdoche, symbolism, and allegory, these last two as with the Biblical application — not the Classical and Romantic — of the terms) and consequently they fall into anthropomorphism whenever they relate Qur'anic references to

---

28. The verses of the Holy Qur'an are traditionally said to be divisible into two categories: *Ahkam* (verses relating to legislation, the sum total of which are known as *Umm al-Kitab*, the "Mother of the Book") and *Akhbar* (verses relating to "parables" or to "wisdom" — all the other verses). By "non-legislative verses" we obviously mean the *Akhbar*.

God.[29] On the legal plane, the fundamentalists reject the last two of the four great traditional Principles of Islamic Jurisprudence (*Usul al-Fiqh*) of Qur'an, *Sunna* (the example of the sayings and actions of the Prophet Muhammad [ﷺ]), *Qiyas* (logical analogy from Qur'an and *Sunna*) and *Ijma'* (the consensus of the sum total of qualified Muslim scholars on a particular issue): i.e., they reject *Qiyas* and *Ijma'*, and this leaves the door open for them to alter any law they like or dislike (a situation which they use according to political convenience). Furthermore, they even go so far as to encroach on the planes of *Tafsir* (Qur'anic Commentary) and *Hadith* (the sayings of the Prophet Muhammad [ﷺ]): on the plane of *Hadith* they have substituted for the traditional canonical books their own politically expedient "revised collections" of *Hadith* by the Shaykh al-Albani and the like; and on the plane of *Tafsir* they deny that the Arabic language is etymologically "fixed" by the fact that every word goes back to a tri-literal root whose meaning has its origin in a natural (and hence desert-related) phenomenon, and

---

29. In the Qur'an, God made man with His "own Spirit" (32:9), and as already quoted, the Prophet Muhammad (ﷺ) said: *God created Adam in His own image* (*Musnad Ibn Hanbal*, I: 251 and *Sahih Muslim*, XLV: 32). Certain fundamentalists, however, believe that God on His Throne in Heaven is like a man, since the Qur'an describes that He has a Hand, a Side, that He is the Hearer, the Seer, etc. Ibn Taymiyyah, referring to a famous *hadith*, said: "God descends from the Heavens, even as I am descending from this *minbar*." In other words, instead of believing that man is made in God's image, the fundamentalists believe that God is like a man (although they say it is forbidden to try to imagine him, which is unfathomable, because the Qur'an says: *God coineth the similitudes for mankind in order that they may reflect* — 14:25).The traditional, orthodox theological position is that the opposite is the case — man is made in God's image — and that there is a double relationship of *Tanzih* (abstraction) and *Tashbih* (similarity) between man and God. If, on the one hand, man reflects God's Attributes, on the other hand, God is infinitely beyond all comparisons, as expressed in the following Qur'anic dialectic:

Nothing is like unto Him, and He is the Hearer, the Seer. (42:11)

semantically "fixed" by the corpus of Classical pre-Islamic poetry; a denial which alone opens the door to "making" the Qur'an itself mean new, heterodox, and potentially dangerous things. Finally, the Islamic fundamentalists are characterized by their rejection of all mention of theology, philosophy, mysticism, traditional psychology; by their rejection of traditional notions of spirituality; by their destruction of sepulchral shrines; by their rejection of the immaculateness, human perfection, and spiritual impeccability of the Prophet (ﷺ) and of the role of his family; and by their militant "puritanism" which seeks not only to condemn followers of other religions, but also everyone in their own religion who does not share their ideas; and by their political activism and their focus on the rhetoric of *Jihad al-Asghar* (the Lesser Holy War — the war against unbelievers) rather than on the *Jihad al-Akbar* (the Greater Holy War — the war against one's own soul). In short, it is obvious that a fundamentalism, if it becomes the dominant movement within a given religion, is quite sufficient to transform that religion into something completely different to what it has always been, and to produce a culture — and perhaps even a civilization — that has little relation to the traditional one issuing from the same source.

Turning now to the fourth cause of the present cultural "disequilibrium and upheaval," it will not escape any student of history if we say that the modern world is unique in that never before have there been no barriers (or so relatively few) to social, racial, religious, or artistic interaction, or to the flow of information and knowledge. In our times everything is known — or can be known — by everyone, for in one's local library, and recently on the Internet, one can find out almost everything ever known from the arcane, magical, and even mystical secrets of ancient religions to cosmetic surgery to how to build an atomic bomb. Nothing is hidden, nothing is secret, nothing is inaccessible, and at any time one can talk to anyone about anything, or indeed, buy anything from anyone. For example, today one can view Mameluke calligraphy; purchase Native American handicrafts; eat Japanese sushi; acquire a reproduction of Delacroix's painting of Hannibal crossing the Alps; watch American "television sitcoms"; listen to Gregorian chants; contemplate Our Lady of Vladimir; practice Hindu Yoga; and wear African clothes all with the same ease and at a relatively low cost. Thus there is, especially in the realms of information exchange and of commercial trade, a kind of "universal flux" which has reduced the whole earth to — if one may be permitted to use a now well-worn phrase — a "global village." This situation, with which we are now all very familiar, and which has been greatly augmented in the last decade by the fall of communism, the collapse of the "iron curtain," and the commercial "opening-up" of China — to say nothing of the proliferation of the "information super-highway" — most assuredly did not exist a few centuries ago. Only a few centuries ago, if, in Europe or in India, one committed the pettiest imaginable social indiscretion, one would legally (and, in practice, usually) receive a thorough drubbing; if one met a person of a different race one would usually try to enslave them; and if one met a person of a non-indigenous religion (or even sometimes of an indigenous but different religion) the "natural thing" would be to try to kill them! Moreover, everywhere in the world and throughout time history before the Renaissance, most people, unless they were nomads, would never leave their village or town in their whole lives, unless they went away for war or for pilgrimage somewhere. Of course, there were merchants and travelers who explored the world,[30] but these were a tiny minority of the population, and

30. When we say "the world" here, we of course mean "the known world" in the Middle Ages, or rather: "those parts of the world known to each other, and not just to their indigenous inhabitants." Thus half of what we know of as the world today — both American continents, both polar regions, Australasia,

most people, being laymen, did not know very much about their own religion and civilization, let alone about other cultures and races. Rather, they were only dimly aware of the existence of these latter, in the much same way that people nowadays are aware of other solar systems: other solar systems, we may well recognize in theory, have suns similar to, or even greater than, our own, but to us they are merely stars in the sky and only our sun is *the* sun. As the popular historian William Manchester says of Medieval Europe, exaggerating only slightly:

> One consequence of medieval peril was that people huddled closely together in communal homes. They married fellow villagers and were so insular that local dialects were often incomprehensible to men living only a few miles away. . . . Each hamlet was inbred, isolated, unaware of the world beyond the most familiar local landmark: a creek, or mill, or tall tree scarred by lightning. There were no newspapers or magazines to inform the common people of great events; occasional pamphlets might reach them, but they were usually theological and, like the Bible, were always published in Latin, a language they no longer understood.[31]

In short, the vast majority of people before modern times were, although certainly not ignorant or unintelligent — as the fruits of their cultures, precisely, prove — nevertheless illiterate laymen,

---

Sub-Saharan Africa, and huge swaths of Asia itself — were not only unknown, but inaccessible due to the perils of land routes and lack of adequate navigational techniques over water. One need only look at the most famous world maps of the ancient and medieval worlds — those of Eratosthenes (200 B.C.), Ptolemy of Alexandria (c. 150 B.C.), and Al-Idrisi (1154 A.D.) — to appreciate this.

31. William Manchester, *A World Lit Only by Fire* (London: Macmillan, 1994), 6, 22.

who were not fully apprised of all of the treasures of their own culture and history and had little real experience or even knowledge of any other.

Thus, the general cultural situation in the modern world is unprecedented in the history of the world in at least four ways: in respect of its having so much secular content;, in respect of what religious content it has being beset by fundamentalism; in respect of its being so interspersed with technology; and in respect of there being so few barriers to the flow and exchange of knowledge and information (and people and wares). These four phenomena together do have one unifying and homogenizing effect, however: they work together against the old "cultural traditions" to create more disorder and confusion on the cultural level than has ever existed before in history. There is so much disparate "culture" bombarding the lives of ordinary people nowadays (including rural populations, through the mediums of television and radio) and such a spate and plethora of information available to the average person — more, indeed, than any one person could fully digest in a single lifetime — that it forms a single amorphous and at times unintelligible mass, whose net effect is to bamboozle the individual with an unstable and unreal panoply of multiplicity. The following lines, written perhaps with remarkable prescience in 1920 by W. B. Yeats, are tellingly often quoted in this respect:

> Turning and turning in the widening gyre
> The falcon cannot hear the falconer;
> Things fall apart; the centre cannot hold;
> Mere anarchy is loosed upon the world. . . .[32]

32. From "The Second Coming," *The Norton Anthology of English Literature*, vol. 2 (New York: Norton, 1993), 1973.

Indeed, however much one masks this situation with euphemisms like "ecumenism," "cosmopolitanism," "globalism," and "universalism," it must nevertheless be admitted that in the center of contemporary culture, superimposed upon the background of the six or seven main, traditional civilizations of the world, lies a fundamental crisis in meaning and order.[33]

33. This is seen above all in the realm of religion, where exposure to the existence and *pertinent reality* of millions, if not billions, of patently sincere and virtuous adherents of other major faiths poses the question: how can all such be damned? Of course, Islam, being the last great world religion, does not face such a problem with this issue, because the Qur'an acknowledges the Heavenly origin and authenticity of its monotheistic predecessors and adds both that: *Verily We have sent Messengers before thee [Muhammad]. About some of them have We told thee, and about some have we not told thee. . . . (40:78) and: And verily We have raised in every nation a Messenger [proclaiming]: serve God and shun false gods. . . .* (16:36). However, it is obviously not so easy for a preceding (true) religion to admit to the authenticity of a later one without also admitting, in good logic, its abrogation by it. This theological conundrum is in a sense directly caused by the breakdown of barriers in the modern world, because in bygone times it was precisely these barriers which allowed the adherents of the other great religions to blissfully assume that everyone not of their faith was evil and damned. . . .

(vii) THE REALITY OF CULTURE TOMORROW

IT WILL COME as no surprise if we now say that "confusion" in culture itself has led to a certain confusion about the future of culture; a confusion that is evident in the widely differing prognosis of culture put forward by the pundits and mandarins of our day. An article in *The Economist* of November 9–15, 1996, entitled "Cultural Explanations," provides a characteristically excellent overview of the contemporary discussion of the issue: basically, at the end of the twentieth century, there are three major positions about the future of culture in the world and a number of minor ones related to these. The first maintains that the six or seven major "cultural traditions" of the world (with some readjustment as to their borders and definitions) will "crystallize" and oppose each other politically; the second, conversely, maintains that these "cultural traditions" will flow into a single unified "world-wide culture" which will be dominated by the Western democratic capitalist system; and the third maintains that the nations of the world will be dominated by two contradictory movements: one — consisting of nations like the United States (or parts of it) — where "modern civilization" continues unabated with technological "progress" and "better" standards of living (but which does not *necessarily* exclude traditional culture), and the other — consisting of nations like Liberia — where society will disintegrate into chaos, anarchy, and villainy.

The first scenario was given intellectual credibility by Harvard Professor Samuel P. Huntington's famous article "The Clash of Civilizations" in the Summer 1993 edition of the influential journal *Foreign Affairs* (by 1996 the article was expanded to a full-length book entitled *The Clash of Civilizations and the Remaking of the World Order*). Huntington's thesis is essentially that the world, having moved, over the course of the twentieth century, through the divisions of nationalism and competing ideologies, is now once again "crystallizing" back into its traditional civilizational and cultural "conglomerations" or blocs; and that as a result of this "recrystallization" the "Islamic" and "Confucian" (Chinese) blocs are going to unite to "battle" against the West. It will be noted, however, that his vision of the major "cultural civilizations" of the world is not identical to the major "religious traditions" of the world, as we defined them earlier: we had spoken of the Jewish, Christian, Islamic, Hindu, Buddhist, Taoist–Confucian, and Shamanist/Animist cultural traditions; whereas Huntington envisages — taking religion into consideration, but also considering history, geography, ethnicity, political alignment, and thus "culture" in a more general way — Western, Orthodox, Latin American, Islamic, Hindu, Buddhist, Sinic, Japanese, and African "civilizational blocs." It will also be noted that for Huntington it is culture that determines "civilization" — a view which, while ignoring the differences between "culture" and "civilization" as discussed earlier on, is nevertheless not without meaning in the sense that culture is the active content of "civilization" — and so for him the future of one is synonymous with the future of the other (even if the scenario is, for him, a turbulent one):

> World politics is entering a new phase, and intellectuals have not hesitated to proliferate visions of what it will be — the end of history, the return of traditional rivalries between nation states from the conflicting pulls of tribalism and globalism, among others. Each of these visions catches aspects of the emerging reality. Yet they all miss a crucial, indeed a central, aspect of what global politics is likely to be in coming years.

It is my hypothesis that the fundamental source of conflict in this new world will not be primarily ideological or primarily economic. The great divisions among humankind and the dominating source of conflict will be cultural. Nation states will remain the most powerful actors in world affairs, but the principal conflicts of global politics will between nations and groups of civilizations.[34]

Huntington's theory is, in a certain sense, the exact opposite of the second major theory about the future: that of Francis Fukuyama of George Mason University in his award-winning book *The End of History and the Last Man*. Although like Huntington Fukuyama sees the future of culture and the future of the world in general as synonymous, his views are at antipodes to Huntington's as to the form these will take: Fukuyama argues that political history has "evolved" into its final and most "perfect" form — Western liberal democracy — and that this form of government is bound by "human evolution" to embrace, ultimately, the whole world. In other words, democracy is the ideology that permits human society to reach its scientific and economic acme, and therefore may be "historically destined" to be irresistible everywhere, and all the "traditional civilizations" are simply going to gradually — if in places fitfully — melt into one universal, homogenous, liberal, capitalist culture:

> Rather than a thousand shoots blossoming into many different flowering plants, mankind will come to seem like a long wagon train strung out along a road. Some wagons will be pulling into town sharply and crisply, while others will be bivouacked back in the desert, or else stuck in the ruts in the final pass over the

---

34. *Foreign Affairs*, Summer 1993 edition, 22.

mountains. Several wagons, attacked by Indians, will have been set aflame and abandoned along the way. There will be a few wagoneers who, stunned by the battle, will have lost their sense of direction and are temporarily heading in the wrong direction. . . . Others will have found alternative routes to the main road. . . . But the great majority of wagons will be making the slow journey into town, and most will eventually arrive there. . . . [If] enough wagons would pull into town . . . any reasonable person looking at the situation would be forced to agree that there had been only one journey and one destiny.[35]

The third major theory about the future — based on another seminal article, in this case, Robert D. Kaplan's "The Coming Anarchy," published in the February 1994 issue of *The Atlantic Monthly* (and later developed into a book entitled *The Ends of the Earth*) — contends that the planet is rapidly destroying itself and that modern society has sown the seeds of its own dissolution through environmental destruction and pollution, famine, disease, droughts, over-population, tribalism, civil war, crime, conflict, and so on. Kaplan also sees huge swaths of the world dying or killing each other, but a few rich and stable societies, who possess the power to defend themselves, surviving what he calls the "Coming Anarchy"; like a modern "Noah's Ark story" based upon economic resources, medicine, and nuclear weapons. Kaplan's future is in a certain sense a cross between Huntington's and Fukuyama's: for him some societies will become more "democratic" and "capitalist" and others will "recrystallize" into their old traditional cultures; perhaps conflict will ensue between these

35. Francis Fukuyama, *The End of History and the Last Man* (Washington, D.C.: National Affairs, 1989), 338–39.

two kinds of societies, and perhaps not. Culture will be a muddled hybrid of the traditional and the "modern democratic," and its inherent resilience in each nation or country will be the decisive determining factor — natural and environmental givens notwithstanding — in the future survival of societies in the impending destruction and turmoil he foresees.

These three theories bear within them more or less the entire gamut of speculations about the future of culture over the next fifty years or so. All three are cogently argued and well-researched, and each has obvious strengths and weaknesses, which can only be briefly mentioned here. To start with, Huntington's scenario of different states uniting and forming "blocs" along cultural lines, and then of the "Islamic bloc" forming an alliance with "Confucian China" which will then clash with the West, sounds highly improbable for the following three reasons: first, even if it is unfortunately true that there is great animosity along cultural lines in the world, it is just as true that there is bitter internecine rivalry — if not also animosity — *within* culturally defined regions, and it is difficult to see people overcoming nationalism, ideology, ethnicity, geography, socio-economic disparity, and religious denominational differences to unite into "cultural blocs." Second, it must be said that Huntington does not seem to differentiate between traditional religion and fundamentalism, and completely ignores the possibility of conflict between the two preventing the crystallization of internally unified cultural blocs. Moreover, fundamentalism is a cultural dead-end, a *cul-de-sac*, which cannot on its own long sustain a civilization and which, for that very reason, can be considered the swan-song of a religion.[36] In other words, fundamentalism cannot

36. The phenomena of religious fundamentalism, which violently and "pharisaically" insists on the "letter" of a religion in the name of "returning it to its original purity" (precisely because it no longer understands its "spirit"), is not to be confused with the "hard asceticism" and "spiritual vigor" of that "original

exist alongside a traditional religious culture without trying to eradicate it. If it does eradicate it, it does so to its own eventual demise
for a religion cannot long survive without a culture to surround and
protect it. And since the phenomenon of fundamentalism shows no
sign of going away of its own accord, one way or another there is
bound to be some internal religious strife, even if only to put an end
to this unhappy phenomenon. Third, it is difficult to see what
monotheistic Islam has more in common with Confucian or
Communist China than it has with the Christian, or perhaps post-
Christian, West; that Huntington should say that are going to make
common cause and "fight" the West is therefore quite puzzling, if
not incomprehensible.

Turning now to Fukuyama's idea of Western liberal democracy pervading everywhere, it must be said that the thesis fails to take
into consideration the spiritual — if not moral — bankruptcy of
this ideology and the social unrest and discontent it can produce.
For the verdict is not yet out on these modern Western societies,
and in particular on the secularism inherent within them, and it
may yet be that despite their economic strength they are not
socially viable in the long term. Moreover, Fukuyama's thesis also

---

purity" itself. What Ibn Khaldun, in his classic on the nature and cycles of traditional civilizations *Al-Muqadimah*, sees as the "first generation" of a religion or of
"a conquering nomadic dynasty" that "renews" a religion, may outwardly manifest the same "fire" and "rigor" that fundamentalism preaches, but internally is
hardly the same. Rather, the former is based upon true inspiration and devotion
— and therefore also mercy — whereas the latter is based upon xenophobia, misunderstanding, and, sometimes even, downright spite. This is sadly all too clearly seen in our day in the acts of terrorism undertaken in the name of various religions of the world, acts to which, needless to say, those religions themselves have
always been implacably opposed. It need hardly be mentioned that Islam, even
in a just, holy war or *jihad*, strictly forbids the harming of non-combatants and
their property — let alone women and children, the elderly, medical personnel,
clerics, and so on, be they Muslims or non-Muslims — and yet modern so-called
"Islamic Fundamentalists" seem to focus on doing precisely that. . . .

smacks of a certain psychological naïvety since it implies a Marxist view of the world, namely that history is determined (or even should be determined) by economic factors, a view which is belied by the fact that men, in particular those belonging to traditional, religious societies, have never acted strictly in accordance with their economic interests alone: the Bible reports that Jesus (ﷺ) said: *Man shall not live by bread alone.*[37]

Taking the flaws of Kaplan's theory next, aside from his Malthusian pessimism, which verges at times on apocalypticness, Kaplan does not discern between the different elements of culture existing in the modern world. He points to the varied and heterogeneous nature of these elements without for all that categorizing them, showing the trends building up in them, explaining their origins, or saying how each in particular will live up to, or crumble under, the environmental pressures he predicts. However, it has to be said that Kaplan's acute awareness of environmental, demographic, and sociological problems is very illuminating and is not found in the others, and that his grasp of the breadth, complexity, and diversity of all the things that make up culture in the "real" world is also impressive.

This leads us to some of the minor, "related" positions on the future of culture, surveyed in the above-mentioned article in *The Economist*. Orientalist-extraordinaire, Professor Bernard Lewis of Princeton University, starts his history of the Middle East by pointing out that even the most die-hard anti-Western fundamentalists wear Western clothes, use Western technology and tote Western guns — all things which are undeniably "Western," even if they were originally developed through learning that came from the East. In other words, there is an extremely complex and "interactive" give-and-take about the sum of culture in the modern world

---

37. Matthew 4:4.

which possesses its own history. If this position shares with Kaplan's an understanding of the complexity of modern culture, Benjamin Barber, by contrast in his *Jihad vs. Mcworld* and Thomas Sowell, in his *Race and Culture; A World View*, share with Huntington certain aspects of his cultural vision of the world and of the conflict looming large within: as the title of his book suggests, Barber sees two great, conflicting cultural currents in the world — universal commercialism and tribalism (*Jihad* indicating, for Barber, not just Islam or Islamic fundamentalism, but also prejudice, fascism, extreme nationalism, and so on — everything which for him threatens "globalism"); these two categories being for him not primarily "nations" or "cultural blocs" but "states of mind," which for all that are still going to "clash"; Sowell, on the other hand points to the role of ethnicity in determining culture, and therefore also economics, politics, and, ultimately, "conflict." Related to Fukuyama's position — in fact pre-dating it considerably, and thus perhaps instrumental in its formulation — is Max Weber's now classical investigation of the Protestant work ethic which showed that culture and economics are deeply intertwined, an idea which can perhaps be accepted without necessarily also taking a Marxist view of history.

Obviously all the positions here have been greatly simplified for the purposes of this monograph, and obviously none of them has a monopoly on the truth or the future: these two perhaps lie somewhere between them all. However, by considering them all together, it was our intention not just to shed light on the future of culture — or even on the culture of the future — but on the nature of culture itself, for speculations about what can happen to it in the future must be inherently instructive about what it is in the present.

(viii) WHAT CULTURE CAN DO

HAVING THUS DISCUSSED what culture is and what it might become, it can now be asked what culture *can* do. Most people nowadays are perhaps familiar with World War II *Luftwaffe* Chief Hermann Goering's famous quip (paraphrasing the poet Hans Johst): "When I hear the word 'culture' I reach for my gun." Most people nowadays only see in it an amusing, if somewhat raw, machismo with which they secretly sympathize in opposition to the pretences and unintelligibility of modern art. Hidden within it, however, lie two greater ideas — ideas which make it in fact worthy to be remembered as much as it is — the first being that culture has a tremendous power, power indeed to rival that of guns; and the second being that culture is a force that scares iniquity and villainy deeply, and therefore one that is a potential vehicle for great moral good. We shall return to this second point in the following section, but as regards the power of culture, it is worth noting the views of the great Renaissance historian, Jacob Burckhardt, in his *Reflections on History*. He saw culture as one of the three reciprocal powers — along with the state and religion — that determines the course of history:

> Its action on the two constants [the state and religion] is one of perpetual modification and disintegration, and is limited only by the extent to which they have pressed it into their service and included it within their aims. Otherwise it is the critic of both, the clock which tells the hour at which their form and substance no longer coincide. Culture is, further, that millionfold process by which the spontaneous, unthinking activity of a race is

transformed into considered action, or indeed, at its last and highest stage, in science and especially philosophy, into pure thought. Its total external form, however, as distinguished from the state and religion, is society in its broadest sense.[38]

Now although we may not necessarily agree with Burckhardt's "linear" view of history nor even of his exact definition of culture as such, we cannot but agree with him about the power latent in culture. Anyone living after the Second World War in the twentieth century will not have failed to observe that American political, economic, technological, and military power — not to say global domination — has gone hand in hand with the dispersion of "Americana" culture, in some form or other, to every nook and cranny in the world. In fact, "Americana" culture has in no small measure contributed to the strength and size of the American economy in the first place (through the export of American products and services) as well as to American political influence (through sympathetic American-educated elites all over the world), and this, despite its youth and relative poverty vis-a-vis the "high cultures" of older civilizations (a youth and relative poverty which Americans, to their credit, are often the first to admit, and which explains why, as quoted earlier, they are so keen to preserve European and other high culture in their museums and libraries). Moreover, it will not have gone unnoticed that the collapse of the Soviet Union — which opposed capitalist countries primarily for ideological and cultural reasons — did not come about through military confrontation, but rather through economic, social, ideological — and therefore ultimately cultural — pressures.

38. Jacob Burckhardt, *Reflections on History* (London: G. Allen and Unwin, 1943), 93. Despite certain nineteenth-century prejudices, this remains a valuable contribution to the study of both culture and history.

Conversely, when Mao Tse-tung wanted to consolidate power in China he realized the best way to do this was to obliterate (high) culture (in so far as such a thing is possible), and so he brought about "The Cultural Revolution." This "Revolution" (1966–69) destroyed the majority of — if not all — museums and pieces of traditional art of any form (which were abundant in China, for it boasts perhaps the oldest continuous civilization in the world and about a quarter of the world's population) but also the majority of libraries and books (except of course Mao's *Little Red Book* and his other writings); musical instruments; games (including chess and cards); sports; teahouses, bars and restaurants; schools; parks; temples; pagodas; tombs; monuments (the Forbidden City only survived because Premier Zhou Enlai sent soldiers to guard it); and even pets — in other words, anything that pertained to "the four olds": "old ideas, old culture, old customs and old habits." The tactic, needless to say, was brutally effective in prolonging Mao's grip on power (which consequently lasted until his death), even if it killed thousands of people in the process,[39] and this alone should tell us that culture possesses an awesome power at least as great as that of armies or of money — which in fact it necessarily antecedes and perhaps even determines *a priori* — and which, if in the short term does not make itself felt as directly as these, nevertheless, in the long term, has no less potent an effect than them, even on the plane of political action which is not even its primary area of focus.

---

39. As the German poet and essayist Heinrich Heine said (*Almansor*, 1.245): "Wherever books are burned, men will follow."

(ix) WHAT CULTURE SHOULD DO

WHAT SHOULD CULTURE do with its great power? The answer to this
is simple. It is the same as the traditional answer to human life
itself, namely that it should work for the truth, goodness and beauty (with both this world *and* the next in view), and thus also their
reflections in the human subjectivity: knowledge, virtue, and joy or
happiness. At the onset of this monograph we quoted, as an epi-
graph, Matthew Arnold's saying that *culture* — or more specifically "high culture" — is *"to know the best that has been said and thought
in the world."* This, indeed, pithily summarizes all these aspirations,
for "the best" is coterminous with nothing if not "the truth, goodness and beauty." Moreover, when a culture does produce "the best
that has been said and thought in the world," it has an incalculable
beneficial effect not only on the societies and / or civilizations it
shapes, but also on all the individual souls it touches, maximizing
the opportunities for all of them to be happy, wholesome, edifying,
productive and constructive, ultimately even predisposing them to
being receptive to the presence of the Spirit. In other words, for
culture to truly be "high" it should be the seamless moral fabric that
surrounds and protects society; that keeps it moderate and tolerant
on the one hand, and on the other hand binds it together firmly
(over and above laws, government, police, and armies); and finally
that, above all, keeps it healthy.

(x) CONCLUSION

IN CONCLUSION, AND by way of postscript, it must be said that while evidently this monograph is perforce too brief to consider the topic of culture thoroughly, it nevertheless hopefully will have been adequate to showing the major dimensions and difficulties of the subject. It will also hopefully have shown not just how important culture itself is, but also how important understanding — and therefore *a fortiori* discussing — it is. Culture is the very envelope in which we journey through life, and to ignore it is to ignore the way in which this journey is proceeding.

THE PHILOSOPHY BEHIND SPORTS

THE ORIGIN, MEANING,
AND NATURE OF SPORTS,
AND THEIR PRACTICE
IN THE MODERN WORLD.

This essay is divided into the following parts:

(i) INTRODUCTION

THIS ESSAY IS by intention a philosophical tract about the profound meaning and thus the potential benefits (and pitfalls) of sports, but is not necessarily of interest to every reader or to every practitioner of sports, because — and we are the first to admit this — the benefits of sports may easily be reaped by someone with no interest in this essay or with philosophy at all. Indeed, it suffices to enjoy sports and to undertake them in a noble and "sporting" manner — precisely — to make the activity entirely worth the time spent on it for both body and soul. However, philosophy (in the traditional and not the modern, profane understanding of the term) is "the love of wisdom" (*philia* meaning "love" in Greek and *sophia* being the Greek for "spiritual wisdom") and thus the immediate subordinate or "handmaid" of theology (*ancilla theologiae*, as it was known in the Middle Ages), the "Queen of the Sciences." Its very *raison d'être* is to explore and make explicit important topics that are not strictly speaking theological in nature (or at least not exclusively so), in order to protect them from misunderstanding and abuse, and in order to deepen appreciation of them. It is thus the aim of this essay to explain the origin, nature, and most profound purpose of sports, in order to make their practice more conscious and deliberate; in order that their full benefits may be better appreciated and more efficiently reaped; and in order that the dangers inherent in their abuse may be avoided.

(ii) THE ORIGIN OF SPORTS

TURNING FIRST TO the question of the origin of sports[1] as such, one can distinguish between two principal approaches to the issue. The first is objective and historical, and the second is subjective and psychological, albeit that these categories overlap in part. In both cases we will not try herein to prove their arguments — a task evidently beyond such a short tract — but rather merely to recount them, illustrating them just enough to render them easily intelligible.

To start off with, then, let it be said that in general the disciplines of history, archeology, anthropology, and literature concur that organized sports had religious origins wherever they are found in the ancient world. The most famous ancient religious rite associated with sports is obviously the Olympic Games, traditionally held to have started in 776 B.C., but which almost certainly began much earlier. They were consecrated to a number of Olympian "gods" (their name being derived from Mount Olympus where they where supposed to reside), notably Zeus, Apollo, and Gaea, and there were also other sports festivals all over Ancient

---

1. The term "sports" usually refers to any physical recreational activity — individual or collective — that involves rules and leads to contest or competition. Here, however, and throughout this essay, we are using the term "sports" in the broadest possible sense, and thus are including activities which are basically just physical training without any rules or competition (such as jogging); ones that are no longer recreational, but rather are in lethal earnestness (such as motor-racing or even boxing); ones that are actually really "arts" or perhaps "sacred sciences" (such as archery and Oriental swordsmanship — see section (iii)); and ones that are not even physical (such as chess — see Appendix A— although this is perhaps the only example of this).

Greece consecrated to Hera, Athena, Ares, and other "gods" and "goddesses."[2] Ancient Rome was no different:

> In classical antiquity games (*ludi*) had a sacred character and therefore became typical expressions of the traditional path of action. *"Ludorum primum initium procurandis religionibus datum,"* wrote Livy. It was considered dangerous to neglect the sacred games (*negligera sacra certamina*); thus, if the state's funds were depleted, the games were simplified but never suppressed. An ancient Roman law required the duoviri, and the aediles to have the games celebrated in honor of the gods. . . . [A]ction took place in the context of material symbols representing higher meanings, so that "the magical method and technique" hidden in the *ludi* (which always began with solemn sacrifices and were often celebrated to invoke divine powers at times of an imminent national danger) could have a greater efficacy. The impetus of the horses and the vertigo of the race through seven rounds, which was also compared with and consecrated to the sun's "journey" in the sky (see Pindar, *Olympian Odes*, 2.50), evoked the mystery of the cosmic current at work in the

---

2. It is worth noting that in these polytheisms, unlike, say, the idolatry of the pre-Islamic Arabs, a doctrine of "the unity of all the gods" — that "all the gods are merely aspects of the One God" — *originally* underlay and underpinned the multiplicity of "the gods." Furthermore, these "gods" themselves, depending on the ontological level of reality at which they were envisaged, are roughly equivalent to, in the Abrahamic Religions, the Divine Names, the Archetypes, or the Archangels, these latter being none other than the loci or centers of manifestation of the Divine Qualities in Creation. Even the concept of "demigod" — with an immortal spirit already "in Heaven" and a human soul and body "on earth" — in the polytheisms might be said to correspond, to some degree to the concepts of Prophets and Saints in the Abrahamic religions, given that *God created man in His own image* (Genesis 1:27).

"cycle of generation" according to the planetary hierar-chy. The ritual slaying of the victorious horse, which was consecrated to Mars, should be connected to the general idea of "sacrifice"; it seems that the force that was consequently unleashed was for the most part directed by the Romans to increase the crops in an occult fashion, *ad frugum eventum.*[3]

Thus sports events were consecrated to the "gods" whose qualities or natures represented the gifts necessary to win those events, and the act of competition was itself the crowning achievement of an esoteric discipline associated with a particular "god" and whose form and inner meaning both had religious significance.

Indeed, Book XXIII of *The Iliad* shows Achilles holding Funeral Games for his fallen companion Patrocles, and, although secular motives are clearly plentiful among the competitors, nev-ertheless they are clearly meant to be sacred in nature, for even the "gods" themselves get involved in them. Moreover, the Ancient Egyptians, whose religion was a "sister religion" to those of Ancient Greece and Rome (as well as to those of Ancient Iraq and India), also had sacred athletic games similar to those of the Olympics in form, albeit perhaps not on such a grand scale. In short, athletic games were a sacred part of the ancient polytheis-tic religions, and since these polytheisms themselves must have been originally monotheistic in nature, athletic games were thus most probably originally an important part of the ancient primor-dial religions.

In addition to the ritual dimension of athletic games, many other forms of "sacred sports" were practiced throughout the

3. Julius Evola, *Revolt against the Modern World*, trans. Guido Stucco (Rochester, Vt.: Inner Traditions, 1996), 129–31.

ancient world. Some of these — the most well-known being per-haps wrestling[4] and archery (Islamic, Zen and otherwise — see next section), Oriental martial arts (including *tai chi*),[5] *yoga* and chess[6] — survive, more or less intact, to this day. However, oth-ers — such as Greek *pankration*, Hellenic stick-fighting, Roman gladiatorial games, Mongol hunting rites, and the jousting and

4 The Bible (Genesis 32:24) mentions that Jacob (علیه السلام) "wrestled" with the Spirit in the form of a man, and Ibn Ishaq mentions that the Prophet Muhammad (ﷺ) was challenged by — and threw — the champion wrestler of Mecca. (Presumably what is in question in the story of Jacob is the "spiritual contraction" of a Prophet before Revelation, in the same way that Islamic tra-dition relates that the Archangel Gabriel squeezed the Prophet (ﷺ) before the Revelation descended upon him.) In an entirely different vein — but one also connected to religion (see previous footnote) — it is said that Hercules was the "god" of wrestling, and that Zeus and Cronus wrestled for mastery over the cosmos.

5. The origin of the Oriental Martial Arts (including Kung Fu, Tae Kwon Do, Tai Chi, Karate, Kendo, Iado, Jodo, and even perhaps Judo, Thai-boxing, Bando, Aikido, and Ju-Jitsu) is usually traced, in various forms, to the Shaolin Boxing Temple of Bodhidharma, the Patriarch of Zen Buddhism. Bodhidharma was an Indian Buddhist monk who first arrived in China in 520 A.D. He was:

> the original propagator of the martial arts concept. . . . [He] studied the attacking techniques of animals and insects and the forces of nature, and combining these with a special breathing technique, he created a basis for a legendary system of weaponless fighting and mental concentration. (*Modern Karate*, Arneil and Dowler [Chicago: H. Regnery, 1975], 10)

> To help them withstand long hours of meditation he taught them breath-ing techniques and exercises to develop both their strength and ability to defend themselves in the remote mountains where they lived. (*The Way of the Warrior*, Reid and Croucher [New York: Overlook Press, 1995], 20)

Indeed, many Masters of martial arts openly avow that the "way of self-protection" is above all a "way of self-perfection" which only stands to reason given the nature of Zen Buddhism in the first place.

6. See section iii for an explanation of the spiritual nature of *yoga*, and see the Appendix A for the spiritual symbolism of chess.

trial by combat of medieval knights (King Henry II of France died in a jousting tournament!) — are now completely extinct. Others still, finally, survive in altered and secular form such as polo, the ancient Japanese ball-game *kemari*, and its Native American sister games, the last of which we now know as American football. Indeed, it could be said that many, if not most, of the older sports practiced today originated as religious rites.

THE SECOND WAY of considering the question of the origin of sports, which is psychological in nature and is thus not constrained by the limits of archeological research, derives from the argument that, since sports are inherently part of man, they must be as old as man is.[7] That it is to say that since sports are a cross between childhood and adulthood, fun[8] and discipline,[9] play and war — witness *par excellence* the field events of athletic games which have their

7. There are reliefs of sports wrestling dating back to Sumer (4000 B.C.), literary references of the "tricks" and "maneuvers" of wrestling on an Akkadian tablet found at Mari dating back to 3700 B.C., and mentions of wrestling in *The Gilgamesh Epic* itself. Moreover, there is a whole hieroglyphic manual of wrestling to be found at Bani Hassan dating back to 2000 B.C. (See Michael B. Poliakoff, *Combat Sports in the Ancient World* [New Haven: Yale University Press, 1987], 26–51.) Thus records of sports are as old as records of civilization itself. However, archeology obviously cannot trace sports back beyond records themselves and so can neither confirm nor deny the idea that sports are as old as man, especially given that sports like wrestling leave no physical traces.

8. The Modern English word "sport" actually comes from the Middle English word *disporter*, meaning "any light-hearted recreational activity." The Middle English word *disporter* in turn comes from the Latin *desporto*, meaning "to carry away," for this is what amusement does: it momentarily carries us away from mundanity. *The New Encyclopaedia Britannica* , 15th ed., vol. 28, 113.

9. Obviously, all sports with rules or which involve training, inherently also involve a certain amount of discipline and self-discipline. It is perhaps also worth pointing out that in the famous *agogé*, the cultural and educational system of ancient Sparta, sports were the central means used to educate, to discipline, and to instill virtue and patriotism into the city's youth and citizenry at large:

roots in preparation for war[10] as well as in religion, as discussed earlier — all of which are obviously endemic to both man and nature (mammals play, ants wage war), then sports themselves, even in their most organized form, must be normative to man and naturally a part of him. Moreover, if sports are naturally part of man, it follows logically that they almost certainly existed long before any extant archeological or historical traces of them. This idea is supported by the fact that sports are linked to religion, for we know from the remains of ritual burial ceremonies, of cave drawings, and of religious totems, that formal religion started as soon as man, that is *Homo sapiens* did, tens — if not hundreds — of thousands of years ago. The idea finds further credence in the fact that sports are also linked to war, which itself is not only found in nature, but also

---

[Ancient] Greek urban culture had been dominated by the gymnasium for centuries. As the centers of physical and literary training, the gymnasia assumed an importance visible today in the immensity of their ruins. Sparta did not stand apart from this trend: the city was studded with gymnasia, which had to be maintained and staffed. Ephebes [Spartan minors] would have made up only a portion of their clientele; the rest were professional athletes and local enthusiasts who could not bear to forsake the camaraderie of ephebic life. (Nigel M. Kennel, *The Gymnasium of Virtue; Education and Culture in Ancient Sparta* [Chapel Hill: University of North Carolina Press, 1995], 47)

10. Michael B. Poliakoff quotes Lucian (*Anacharis*, 15, 300) in his *Combat Sports in the Ancient World*, 96

We train the youth in sport] not only for the sake of the contests, so that they may be able to take the prizes — since few indeed out of all of them achieve those ends — but to obtain something greater for the whole city and for the youths themselves. For a certain other contest lies before all the good citizens . . . that is to say, freedom for each person individually and for the state in general, and wealth and glory. . . . These are the things [i.e., for our city and that we will live in freedom through them, conquering our enemies if they should attack, and instilling fear into our neighbours, to the extent that most of them cower before us and pay us tribute.

67

in man as conceived in religious terms: not only in the idea of the inner and outer *Jihads*[11] of the various world religions, but also in the universal mythological accounts of ancient wars between angels, "heroes," or *devas* on the one hand, and demons, "monsters," titans, or *asuras*, on the other.[12]

This idea can, moreover, be reconciled with the lack of concrete archeological proof to support it. For a broad survey of ancient religions reveals that every morally legitimate and natural act in which man engages can be — and often was — incorporated into a religious rite.[13] For example, in the *Hajj* (pilgrimage) of

11. The Prophet Muhammad (ﷺ) said, on returning to Medina from a military campaign:

"We have returned from a lesser Jihad to a greater Jihad." The people said: "O Messenger of God, what Jihad could be greater than struggling against the unbelievers with the sword?" He replied: "Struggling against the enemy in your own breast." (Al-Ghazali, *Ihya 'Ulum Al-Din*, 3:14; also quoted in Bayhaqi's *Kitab al-Sunan al-Kubra*.)

Similarly, the New Testament says (Matthew 11:12):

The kingdom of heaven suffereth violence, and the violent take it by force.

12. Even the Book of Genesis mysteriously alludes to such primordial struggles between early races (6:1–8):

And it came to pass that men began to multiply on the face of the earth, and daughters were born unto them, . . . There were giants in the earth in those days. . . . And God saw that the wickedness of man was great. . . . And the Lord said: I will destroy man whom I have created from the face of the earth. . . . But Noah found grace in the eyes of the Lord.

13. One can distinguish, in the realm of religion, between acts that are merely consecrated to God and acts that themselves constitute a religious rite, either through spiritual contemplation of that act or due to the intrinsically holy content of the act itself. For example, in Islam one may consecrate the act of reading a (necessarily noble) book to God by starting it with the *Basmallah* ("In the Name of Allah, the Compassionate, the Merciful"), but reading the Qur'an is in itself an actual prayer or religious rite, due to its Divine nature. The same applies, *mutatis mutandis*, in Christianity as regards eating vis-à-vis receiving the Sacrament of the Eucharist.

Islam, the Muslim pilgrim must perform certain ancient rites which do not form part of his normal daily duties and which he would not usually think of as forms of prayer. These include walking itself (circumambulating the Ka'ba); running (between the rocks of Safa and Marwah); merely looking at the Ka'ba; touching (the Black Stone); throwing pebbles (at Iblis); standing (on Mount Arafah); drinking (water from Zamzam); shaving one's head; sacrificing an animal (a garlanded sheep at the end of the pilgrimage); putting on and wearing certain ritual garments (the *Ihram*), and, above all, coming to and being in a certain sacred place (that is, Mecca). Most people, and even most Muslims, think of prayer as only ritual prayer (*salat*) or personal supplication (*du'a*), but the Prophet (ﷺ) himself said:

> The circumambulating round the Holy House, the passage to and fro between Safa and Marwah, and the throwing of pebbles were only ordained as a means of remembering God.[14]

INDEED, AN IMPARTIAL study of what we know of religions throughout history suggests that such diverse activities as breathing (Hinduism), eating (Christianity), drinking (Christianity), not eating (i.e., fasting in Islam), working (Hinduism), abstaining from work (Judaism), hunting (Native American religions), cultivating the soil (ancient Mediterranean religions), dancing (Hinduism), singing (Christianity), playing music (Christianity), sweating (Native American religions), making love (Hinduism), circumcising (Judaism), washing (Islam), sitting in certain positions (Hinduism), hearing (Hinduism), seeing (Hinduism), reciting (Islam), doctoring (Native American religions), burying (Islam), weaving (Buddhism), smoking (Native American religions), arranging flowers (Buddhism), and even preparing tea (Buddhism)

14. Al-Tirmidhi, *Sunan, Kitab Al-Hajj*, 64.

were all originally not only consecrated to God, but also used as integral parts of various religious prayer rites.

> [I]n a traditional society every necessary activity can also be the Way, and . . . in such a society there is nothing profane; a condition the reverse of that to be seen in secular societies, where nothing is sacred. We see that even a "sport" may also be a "yoga," and how the active and contemplative lives, outer and inner man can be unified in a single act of being in which both selves cooperate.[15]

Thus, since almost every conceivable natural activity was used in these religious rites from pre-historical times (including waging war itself, that is, until Sargon I, around the year 2300 B.C., freed himself of ethical and ritual constraints about the limits of warfare and thereby created the Akkadian empire, the first "world empire" and "the world's first predatory transnational tyranny"),[16] it follows logically that sports, too, existed as part of the primordial religions long before our earliest historical records of them.

> [I]t is an error to believe that in such cases the purely profane usage came first and subsequently suggested the idea of ritual use. This is actually a reversal of the normal relationships, a reversal which moreover conforms to modern conceptions, but to these only, and which it is quite illegitimate to attribute to ancient civilisations. In fact, in every strictly traditional civilisation, all things necessarily start from the principle or from what is closest to it, to descend from there to more and more

15. A. K. Coomarswamy, *What Is Civilisation?*, 149.

16. Robert L. O'Connel, *Of Arms and Men* (New York: Oxford University Press, 1984), 38.

contingent applications; and even these are never considered from the profane point of view which is, as we have often explained, only the result of a degeneration whereby the awareness of their attachment to the principle has been lost.[17]

As further evidence, we quote the following words of a famous Native American holy man, whose monotheistic "natural" religion is perhaps as close to the Primordial Religion as any we know of today. He is explaining a religious rite that no doubt, in some form, is the origin of American football and perhaps, indirectly, rugby:

> There was, until recently, a game among our people which was played with a ball, four teams and four goals which were set up at four quarters. But there are only a few of us today that understand why the game is sacred, or what the game originally was long ago, when it was not really a game, but one of our most important rites. This rite I am going describe now, for it is the seventh and last sacred rite of this period given to us, through a vision, by *Wakan-Tanka* [literally "the Great Spirit"].
>
> The game as it is played today represents the course of a man's life, which should be spent in trying to get the ball, for the ball represents *Wakan-Tanka*, or the [Sacred] Universe [i.e., Heaven], as I shall explain later. In the game it is very difficult to get the ball, for the odds — which represent ignorance — are against you, and it is only one or two of the teams who are able to get the ball and score with it. But in the original rite everybody was

17. René Guénon, *Fundamental Symbols*, trans. Alvin Moore (Cambridge, Eng.: Quinta Essentia, 1995), 142–43.

able to have the ball, and if you think about what the ball represents, you will see that there is much truth in it.[18]

Thus it may be said that whichever way we consider the origin of sports — historically or psychologically, objectively or subjectively — we cannot escape the conclusion that they were originally religious and spiritual in nature and that they are at least as old as recorded history.

18. J. E. Brown, quoting Black Elk, in *The Sacred Pipe: Black Elk's Account of the Seven Rites of the Oglala Sioux* (Harmondsworth: Penguin, 1971), 127–28.

(iii) MYSTICISM IN SPORTS

SUCH, THEN, IS the origin of sports. In this section, prior to discussing the nature and benefits of sports in general, we will discuss how a certain category of special sports are used in mystic "rites" in certain religions. Before that, however, it is necessary to elaborate on two points without which neither mysticism nor sports can be fully understood, namely, what constitutes man from the spiritual point of view, and the difference between religion and mysticism.

TURNING FIRST TO "spiritual anthropology," although it is evident that the subject cannot be fully addressed in such a short space, it can be said that, basically, man is a unity composed of three "concentric" dimensions (and the "points of connection" between them): the Spirit, the soul, and the body. In Christianity these were known as *spiritus*, *animus*, and *corpus*; in Islam they were known as *ruh*, *nafs*, and *jism*; and in the Pythagorean–Platonic tradition they were known as *pneuma*, *psyche*, and *soma*. Indeed, even if this basically tri-part view of man is nowadays more or less unknown, it was — *mutatis mutandis* and with different shades of emphasis — unanimously recognized all over the pre-Renaissance world, and even throughout time and history (which stands to reason, since man is the same everywhere and since religions all address the same fundamental elements).

Explaining and defining our terms and their meanings briefly, let it first be said that the relationship of the soul to the body is like

73

that of a captain to his ship: it is the immortal "inner witness" or the "determining consciousness," which separates from it at death.[19] The spirit is, in turn, the eternal, celestial "inner witness" of the body and soul taken together. The individual spirit is "contained" in the Spiritual World (the *World of the Domination* of Christianity; the *'Alam al-Jabarut* of Islam), but strictly speaking the spirit *is* also the Spiritual World, for in this world there is no separation between subject, object, and their union (nor, indeed, between the knower, the known, and knowledge; the lover, the beloved, and love and so on). However, individual souls are contained *distinctively* in the intermediary Subtle World or the World Soul (the World of the Dominion of Christianity; the *'Alam al-Malakut* of Islam) in much the same way as individual bodies are contained in the World Body or Physical Universe (the Corporeal World; the *'Alam al-Mulk wal Shahadah* of Islam).

Now these three "macrocosmic worlds" (the World Body, the World Soul, and the World Spirit) are, on their own planes, images of each other. They are *a priori* images of God in exactly the same that man (and his three microcosmic worlds: the body, the soul, and the spirit) is. We have already quoted Genesis (1:27) *God created man in His own image*; it remains to be said that Prophet Muhammad (ﷺ) also said: *Verily God created Adam in His own image.*[20] Moreover, since both the macrocosm and microcosm are

---

19. The soul is, of course, said to be reunited with a reconstituted body "in the Spirit" — on Judgment Day, in the "Glorious Resurrection." Between that time and the time of death, however, the soul exists "in the grave" (which is actually none other than the World Soul) where it experiences a foretaste of its final end, felicitous or damned, in "psychic" or "subtle" mode. The Prophet (ﷺ) said: *The grave is either one of Paradise's meadows or one of hellfire's pits.* (Quoted from Imam Al-Haddad, *The Lives of Man*, trans. Al-Badawi [Louisville, Ky: Fons Vitae, 1998], 44.)

20. *Musnad Ibn Hanbal*, 2:244, 251, 315, 323ff; *Sahih Bukhari, Kitab Al-Isti'than*, 1, et al.

"in the image" of God, it follows that they are "in the image" of each other. This, of course, is only logical since when man creates something it inevitably reflects him (or her) in some way or another, and the more perfect that particular creation is, the more perfectly it reflects him or her. Thus, since the world and man are both "full images"[21] of God, they are also necessarily mirror-images of each other. We do not want to dwell too much on this idea here — that "the universe is a large man, and man is a small universe" — since it is a complex one which holds true in innumerable ways, except to say that it forms the substance of an esoteric doctrine known to all religions,[22] and that obviously it also forms the doctrinal basis of traditional astrology (which proposes to relate man's condition by observing that of universe).

21. The Holy Qur'an says (1:31–33):

And He taught Adam all the names, then showed them to the angels, saying: Inform me of the names of these, if ye are truthful. / They said: Be glorified! We have no knowledge saving that which Thou hast taught us. Lo! Thou, only Thou, art the Knower, the Wise. / He said: O Adam! Inform them of their names, and when he had informed them of their names, He said: did I not tell you that I know the secret of the heavens and the earth?

Now "the names" are said to be the Divine Names and thus the Divine Qualities. Knowing them all presupposes being them all, or rather being in their "full image," for one cannot know something for which one does not already have the capacity. As already mentioned, the angels are loci of manifestation of *particular* qualities, and hence they do not know the *all* the names.

22. It is expounded with particular clarity in the ninth principle of Hermes Trismegistos's *Emerald Tablet*, which says: "Thus the little world [man] is created according to the prototype of the great world [the cosmos]," (trans. from Titus Burckhardt's *Alchemy*, [Louisville, Ky.: Fons Vitae, 1997], 197). More important, however, is the following verse from Holy Qur'an, which implies the same thing, especially bearing in mind that God Himself is the Truth: *We shall show them Our Portents on the horizons and within themselves until it will be manifest unto them that it is the Truth* (41:53).

Returning to the three "dimensions" of man as such, it remains to be said that they have, as might be expected, "points of connection" or "nexus" between them. These are usually said to be three: that between the spirit and the soul, that between the soul and the body, and that between all three of them. The "point of connection" between the spirit and the soul is usually referred to as the "Heart"; the "point of connection" between the body and the soul is called *anima*; and the "divine ray" that transpierces all three "parts" of man (and their "points of connection") is called the (uncreated) "Intellect."[23]

The Heart, which is the "point of connection" between the soul and the spirit as such, is thus "the door" to *The kingdom of God* [which] *is within you* (Luke 17:21); it is none other than the *Strait gate . . . which leadeth unto life* but which *few there be that find it* (Matthew 7:14 — "The kingdom" and "life" both evidently being the Spiritual World). Moreover, the reason *few there be that find it*

---

23. By the "uncreated Intellect" we mean of course the "Intellect" in the Neo-Platonic sense (*Nous*). Here it is conceived of as the microcosmic equivalent of Revelation, or "a ray that emanates" from the Sun of the Spirit, and even from "the Divine Self," right down to the material world and to the body. We evidently do not mean the "intellect" as understood in the modern sense, where it basically means little more than the rational intelligence and the memory:

> It is important above all not to confuse Intellect and reason: the latter is indeed the mental reflection of the transcendent Intellect. But in practice it is only what one makes of it, by which we mean that, in the case of the modern sciences, its functioning is limited by the empirical method itself; at the level of the latter, reason is not so much a source of truth as a principle of coherence. (T. Burckhardt, *The Mirror of the Intellect* (Cambridge, England: Quinta Essentia, 1987), 48; 48; 46 respectively.)

It is interesting, moreover, to note that the Arabic word *Aql*, which in the Qur'an means the Intellect as explained above, has nowadays in Modern Arabic also been reduced to mere reason.

is, in Islamic terms now, precisely that, in the case of the majority of people, *It is not the eyes that are blind but the Hearts* (The Holy Qur'an 22:46).[24] In short, the Heart is none other than the "third eye" that the mystic way universally[25] seeks to "open" so that, through inner vision, the mystical consciousness before may "enter" the world of the Spirit. We quote the following words of a Native American "holy man":

> [I]t is the wish of the Great Spirit (*Wakan Tanka*) that the light enters into the darkness that we may see not only with our two eyes, but with the one eye which is of the Heart (*Chante Ishta*), and with which we see and know all that is true and good.[26]

As to the "point of connection" between the body and the soul, it will be noted that whereas the body is obviously mortal, and is composed of a "gross" or "physical" substance, the soul, as Aristotle puts it, is "immortal and perpetual,"[27] and is composed of

---

24. The doctrine of the Heart is clearly summarized in Islam by the following *Hadith Qudsi*:

My earth hath not room for Me, neither hath My sky, but the Heart of believing slave hath room for Me. (Al-Ghazali, *Ihya 'Ulum Al-Din*, III.1.5; 12.)

We note that here, God "includes" Himself as "within" His "kingdom," because, following the symbolism of monarchy (which is also used in Islam, and particularly in the Qur'an where (59:23) one of the Divine Names is *Al-Malik*, "The King") that is where "a king" is found. Obviously, however, in this case, the King is infinitely greater than His "kingdom."

25. The doctrine of the Heart is to be found, *mutatis mutandis*, in most of history's intrinsically orthodox religions. As evidence of this we refer the reader to two masterly articles by A. K. Coomaraswamy entitled "Symplegades" and "*Janua Coeli*" in Selected Papers Vol. 1: *Traditional Art and Symbolism*, ed. Lipsey (Princeton, N.J.: Princeton University Press, 1977).

26. J. E. Brown, quoting Black Elk, in *The Sacred Pipe: Black Elk's Account of the Seven Rites of the Oglala Sioux*, 42.

27. Aristotle, *De Anima*, trans. Hugh Lawson–Tancred (Baltimore: Penguin, 1987), III.6, 205.

a "subtle" substance. Souls are contained in the "World Soul," just as bodies are contained in the "World Body" or "physical world," and the former is much vaster than the latter which in fact issues from it and is immersed in it like a crystal forming in a bowl of water. The relationship of an individual soul to its body is thus like that of a rider to his horse: he determines it and cares for it, for he cannot move without it in the world. However, it is even more than this because what affects the body is "felt" directly by the soul, not unlike the way a pregnant mother feels the stirrings of the foetus within her womb. Now there are a number of traditional doctrines that explain how this "feeling" occurs: the ancient Hindus speak of seven "chakras" or points along the body through which soul and body are "connected"; Medieval Europe thought in terms of "humors" which were common to body and soul; the Alchemists and Hermetists referred to *anima* as the link between the soul (*animus*)[28] and the body; certain people in the modern world have talked of an "astral body" which is perhaps the same idea, and finally, in Islam, Ghazali (for one) speaks cryptically about a "cavity" within the physical heart where the soul is mysteriously and subtly "connected" to the body.[29] Thus, there is a kind of "umbilical chord" wherein the soul and the body meet (and which, in a certain manner, "partakes" of both their natures) and which is lost at death or shortly after, and it is precisely this that Descartes[30] was unclear about when he started formulating the

28. The term "animus" is not to be confused with "Animus," which is synonmymous with the term "spirit."

29. Al-Ghazali, *Ihya 'Ulum Al-Din*, III.3.

30. Descartes appears to be in a difficult position. On the one hand, his application of the criterion of clarity and distinctiveness leads him to emphasize the real distinction between the soul and the body and even to represent each of them as being a complete substance. On the other hand, he does not want to accept the conclusion which appears to follow, namely, that the soul is simply lodged in the body which it uses as a kind of extrinsic vehicle or instrument. And he did not reject this conclusion simply to avoid criticism on theological grounds.

idea of a mind–body "duality." It is also in fact this same "umbilical chord" that religions seek to "appease" through their rites for the dead (the immortal soul itself goes to where it is going immediately after death) for otherwise this "umbilical chord" can "thrash" around in the world for a great length of time, especially if the death of the person in question was violent or one for which that person was unprepared. In these cases the "psychic remains" of the "umbilical chord" is known as a "ghost" — precisely as in the play *Hamlet* — and it is this phenomenon that explains why in Islam the only sin for which the whole community can be held responsible without knowing of its existence is not praying for the dead: if prayer rites are not said for those dead who need them, the whole community inevitably suffers from, and with, its "ghosts."[31]

For he was aware of empirical data which militate against the truth of the conclusion. He was aware, in other words, that the soul is influenced and the body by the soul and that they must in some sense constitute a unity. He was not prepared to deny the facts of interaction, and, as is well known, he tried to ascertain the point [sic] of interaction. . . . [But physical] localization of the point of interaction does not, indeed, solve the problems arising in connection with the relationship between an immaterial soul and a material body; and from one point of view seems to underline the distinction between soul and body. (Frederick Copleston, S.J., *A History of Philosophy*, book 2, vol. 4 [New York: Image Books, 1985], 121–22.)

31. It is perhaps also worth mentioning, in this context, that within the "general scheme" of the "connections" between the soul and the body there is a particular "nexus" between the soul and the physical brain and that this "nexus" is none other than what we call the "mind":

Mechanists consider mind to be part of the body, but this is a mistake. The brain is part of the body, but mind and body are not identical. The brain breathes mind like lungs breathe air. . . . The soul is the final locus of our individuality. Situated, as it were, behind the senses, it sees through the eyes without being seen, hears through the ears without itself being heard. Similarly, it lies deeper than mind. If we equate mind with the stream of consciousness, the soul is the source of this stream; it is also its witness while never itself appearing within the stream as a datum to be observed. (Huston Smith, *Forgotten Truth* [New York: Harper and Row, 1976], 63, 74.)

Turning back now to the faculties — and thus the nature — of the soul as such,[32] it must first be said that the subject is an extremely complex one, and has naturally occupied much of human inquiry over history. However, it is also one which bears a cursory investigation of it here, especially since it is possible to depict a rough consensus over it — at least as far as traditional religion and philosophy are concerned — for man is everywhere the same, particularly in his religious behavior.[33] Thus let it be said, as a starting point, that Plato describes the different basic constituent parts of the soul (from which arise the soul's basic "emotions") as follows:

> As to the soul's immortality, then, we have said enough, but as to its nature there is this that must be said. . . . Let it be likened to the union of powers in a team of winged steeds and their winged charioteer. . . . [I]t is a pair of steeds that the charioteer controls; moreover, one of them is noble and good, and of good stock, while the other has the opposite character, and his stock is opposite. Hence the task of our charioteer is difficult and troublesome.[34]

Now this basic tri-part schema — the rational soul (the charioteer); the bad steed (the ego); the good steed (the conscience) — is,

32. The faculties of the body as such are not mentioned above because they are evidently none other than its physical capabilities, internal bodily sensations and the five senses; those of the Spirit are evidently both infinite and ineffable.

33. For an excellent general introduction to "the directions and possibilities that lie before the soul" and its general nature as viewed in "diverse traditional contexts" see Alvin Moore's essay "The Noble Traveler" in the May 1996 issue of *Parabola* on "The Soul."

34. Plato, *Phaedrus*, trans. R. Hackforth (Indianapolis: Bobbs–Merril, 1952), 246 a–b.

mutatis mutandis, the same all over the traditional world, notwith-standing the medieval debates in Islam and Christianity about whether these "parts" can be considered "separate souls" or parts of the same soul. Indeed, the Qur'an distinguishes between a "soul at peace" (*al-nafs al-mutma'innah*); a "soul that blames" (*al-nafs al-lawammah*); and "a soul that incites unto evil" (*al-nafs al-ammarah bil-su'*). Even Freudian psychology has a tri-part schema (id, ego, and superego), and while these last two components correspond more or less to Plato's "bad" and "good" steeds respectively, the "id" — with its "impulses" and "internal chatter" — corresponds not to the charioteer or "soul at peace" as such, but to this part of the soul when it has not been "touched" by the Heart or the Spirit, and even when it is shorn of access to its own innate "virtues" by an accumulation of sin, vice, and "psychic rubble." In this state Islamic scholars have called it "the ani-mal soul" (*al-nafs al-haywaniyyah*), that is, "the soul passively obedient to physical and lower impulses," and it is unfortunately only in this state that Freud observed it and classified it as the "id."

Turning now to the actual faculties *per se* of the soul, it should first be stated that the soul has three main "modes" of "perception":

> [M]an is made of intelligence, will and sentiment. . . . [This] means that he is made for the Truth, the Way and Virtue. In other words: intelligence is made for compre-hension of the True; will, for concentration on the Sovereign Good; and sentiment for conformity to the True and the Good.[35]

35. F. Schuon, *Having a Center* (Bloomington, Ind.: World Wisdom Books, 1990), 56. Indeed, both Christianity and Islam share this fundamental concep-tion of the soul of man. St. Paul says: *And now abideth faith, hope, charity, these three* . . . (Corinthians 13:13), and the Holy Qur'an says of the Prophet Muhammad (☆) (48:8): *Lo! We have sent thee as a witness and a bearer of good tidings and a warner.* . . . In the first case faith relates to the intelligence in the

Each of these "modes" — "intelligence," "will," and "sentiment" — then divides into an "essential quaternary" consisting basically of "objective," "subjective," "prospective," and "retrospective" poles[36]: for example, intelligence comprises reason which is objective, intuition which is subjective, imagination which is prospective, and memory which is retrospective. On a different plane, these "modes" can also be subdivided into different "functions" and "aptitudes":

> It is necessary to distinguish in the human spirit between functions and aptitudes: in the first category, which is more fundamental, we shall distinguish between discernment and contemplation, and then between analysis and synthesis; in the second category, we shall distinguish between an intelligence that is theoretical and another that is practical, and then between one that is spontaneous and another that is reactive, or again between an intelligence that is constructive and another that is critical. From an entirely different standpoint, it is necessary to distinguish between a cognitive faculty that is merely potential, another that is virtual and a third that is effective: the first pertains to all men, thus also to the most limited; the second concerns men

---

sense that it pertains to "knowing" even if *through a glass darkly*; hope relates to the will in the sense that they both "project" a good; and charity evidently pertains to sentiment. In the second case the quality of "witness" pertains to certainty and thus *a fortiori* to knowledge; bearing good tidings pertains to sentiment since it brings happiness; and warning involves the will through fear.

36. The "essential quaternary" can just as easily be subdivided into "static," "dynamic," "active," and "passive" poles, or even into the "qualities" of "cold," "hot," "dry," and "wet." They apply symbolically to the four cardinal directions, the four seasons, etc. (in the following order: north, south, east, west; winter, summer, spring, autumn). See F. Schuon, *Esoterism as Principle and Way* (Middlesex, Eng.: Perennial Books, 1990), 65–78, 93–100.

who are uninformed but capable of learning; the third coincides with knowledge.[37]

The three primary "modes of perception" also each comprises an "adjunct" which, as it were, is a kind of further extension of each "mode" in the soul. These are the linguistic faculty, the "creative-and-mimetic" faculty, and the capacity to act. Evidently, the linguistic faculty "extends" and "communicates" the directives of the intelligence; the capacity to act "extends" and "realizes" the directives of the will; and the creative-and-mimetic faculty "extends" and "expresses" sentiment (in the sense that both are concerned with beauty of various forms, and in that love invariably involves creation and imitation, if only in mental constructs and in forms of behavior).

Finally, it perhaps needs to be said that what Jung calls "the collective unconscious" with its so-called "archetypes" is actually only one of the psychic layers in the "nether regions" of the soul. The true "archetypes do not belong to the psychic realm, but to the pure Spirit,"[38] and therefore the patterns Jung identified are actually only the inverted and chaotic reflections of the true, spiritual archetypes in the psyche. Equally, that part of the soul identified by Rank's studies with psychedelic drugs is only another a psychic layer at the "nether regions" of the soul (called the "perinatal" layer), and that part of the soul identified by Freud empirically, through experiments with people under hypnosis, is a third layer in the depths of the soul (called the "psychodynamic"[39] layer). Needless to say, however, it is the three basic "constituent parts" and the three basic modes of perception that are important in the

37. F. Schuon, *Roots of the Human Condition* (Bloomington, Ind.: World Wisdom Books, 1990), 3–4.

38. T. Burckhardt, *Mirror of the Intellect*, 59; see 45–67.

39. Huston Smith, *Forgotten Truth* (HarperSanFrancisco, 1993), 169; see 155–73.

soul — and not the psychic substrata just mentioned — particularly in the "purified" or "sanctified" soul (i.e., one that is "touched" by the Spirit), where these substrata are transformed in such a way that they reflect and express, rather than obstruct and distort, the life of the Spirit.

TURNING NOW TO the difference between religion and mysticism, it must be stated that a religion — from the Latin *religio*, meaning to "bind" (earth to Heaven; man to God) — is a revealed set of moral teachings and (usually) sacred laws through which man learns about God, his own true theomorphic nature (and thus the meaning of his life), his ultimate end, either in Heaven or in hell, and how to influence this end through belief, prayer, shunning evil deeds, and performing good ones. A religion thus occupies itself with purifying the souls of a whole sector of humanity and is thus necessarily exoteric and accessible. As such it also necessarily has to concern itself with regulating social behavior in such a way as to induce the maximum of "moral equilibrium" in human society with a view to facilitating salvation for the maximum possible number of souls.

Mysticism, on the other hand — from the Latin *mysticus* and the Greek *mustikos* meaning a person who had been initiated into the Greek Mysteries — is, in the proper sense of the term an entirely esoteric discipline; it is "something holy and numinous, a secret wisdom"[40]; it is the arcane lore that is necessarily within and part of every authentic religion, both as a prolongation and an intensification of it, and also in opposition to it in the sense that it is not concerned primarily with the religion's normal social and legislative functions, but rather with teaching men and women how to thoroughly purify their souls and how to go beyond that to

40. F. C. Happold, *Mysticism: A Study and Anthology* (Baltimore: Penguin Books, 1963), 18.

the (subtle) Heart, to the Spirit, to Divine Knowledge or *Gnosis*, and then ultimately to Mystic Union. Indeed, the very etymology of the word "arcane" — from the Latin *arcanus* meaning knowledge that is "hidden" or "secret," and the Latin *arca* meaning "chest" (the "home" of the Heart) — suggests at once these three ideas: a teaching that is secret and that relates to the Spirit.

Before modern times mysticism was secret, in all religions and at all times. This was for two reasons. First, because mysticism is not necessary in order that man may find salvation — that is the role of religion — it is only for those whose nature compels them, beyond finding salvation (which only requires the perfection of the soul *virtually* or at least *in intention*)[41] to seek sanctity in this life (i.e., to pass beyond the "world of the soul" into the world of the

---

41. There are those who hold that only God is perfect; while obviously this is true in an absolute sense, it is also true that the soul can reach perfection in a relative sense, and this in fact is the *sine qua non* of sanctity and holiness in the soul. Were this not the case Jesus (ﷺ) would not have said: *Be ye therefore perfect, even as your Father which is in Heaven is perfect* (Matthew 5:48). The reason why this is possible, as already mentioned, God made it *in His own image* (according to Genesis 1:27 and to *hadith*) and because perfection of soul does not necessarily mean perfect "actions" (which evidently are contingent upon exterior circumstances) but only perfect "intentions." Thus the Prophet (ﷺ) said: *Verily acts are* [accomplished] *in their intentions, and each person gets what he* [or she] *intended* (*Sahih Bukhari, Kitab Al-Iman*, 41 et al.). In fact, in order to attain unto "perfection of soul" all a person has to do is purify his or her soul of its sins, faults, and blemishes, because, as we have just mentioned, the soul in itself was created intrinsically perfect:

> The path of "assuming the characters traits of God" does not involve a gradual in stature until people become demigods rivaling God Himself. On the contrary, this path brings about a gradual decrease until human attributes cease to exist, or until people become "nothing." But "nothing" is what belongs to them in the first place. . . . Once they eliminate their own attributes and efface their own selves, there remains only that which is truly found. (William Chittick, *Imaginal Worlds; Ibn al-Arabi and the Problem of Religious Diversity* [Albany: State University of New York Press, 1994], 36–37.)

Spirit). Second, because mysticism is a complex and difficult endeavor which requires special gifts and a particular vocation to understand, let alone practice. Keeping it secret protects the unqualified from its erroneous practice and the qualified from the suspicions and resentment of the unqualified. Thus did one of the Prophet's (ﷺ) close companions, Abu Hurayrah, say: *I have treasured in my memory two stores of knowledge which I had from the Messenger of God. One of them I have made known; but if I divulged the other ye would cut my throat.*[42] It is, however, the most unqualified of all — the profane — that Jesus (ﷺ) doubtless had in mind when he said: *Give not that which is holy unto the dogs, neither cast ye your pearls before swine, lest they trample them under their feet, and turn again and rend you* (Matthew 7:6).

However, with the onset of the Renaissance — and particularly with the advent of the printing press and mass publication in the wake of the Erasmus — documents about mysticism began to make their way into the hands of the general public in the West. Initially, it was the Classical, Greek and Roman texts — notably the Pythagorean and Neo-Platonic traditions (both Plato, and, in particular, Plotinus are quite explicit about mystic experiences) — that gave the reading public their first taste of mysticism, but then Christian mystic texts soon followed and became quite well known to laymen and scholars alike. By the turn of the twentieth century enquiry into mysticism as an autonomous phenomenon within religions had already started[43]: William James, in his *The Varieties of*

42. *Sahih Bukhari, Kitab Al-'Ilm*, 41.
43. Although mysticism differs in both form and in content from religion to religion, and although there are said to be different "kinds" of mysticism even within the same religion (*inter alia* a "mysticism of love," a "mysticism of knowledge," a "mysticism of action"), and although, finally, the spiritual "stations" and "states" can differ from mystic to mystic, it is nevertheless acknowledged that mystical experience is relatively homogeneous everywhere, and shares enough common characteristics to be thought of and studied as the same single

Religious Experience, published in 1902, identifies, despite some pseudo-scientific methodological mistakes, four characteristics typical of mystical experience: "ineffability," a "noetic quality," "transiency," and "passivity."[44] Soon all the major mystic writings of the three "monotheistic" religions, made their way, in translation, to every large library in the world. The Oriental mysticisms, however (and in particular Zen Buddhism whose teachings are not doctrinally formulated but "oral" and "operative") — the only ones where sports were and are still, to this day, an integral part of their mystic "rites" — remained far more laconic until the publication of Eugen Herrigel's seminal *Zen in the Art of Archery* in the 1950s.

IN THIS LITTLE book, Herrigel, a German professor of philosophy, relates how he was initiated, step by step, over six years into Zen mysticism through the practice of traditional archery. In less than one hundred short pages Herrigel opens up — clearly and completely — to humanity an entire world that had hitherto been more or less unknown, not just to non-Orientals but to Oriental non-Buddhist practitioners alike, and in this sense his little book is one of the few this century which has genuinely contributed to the history of knowledge. He explains the object of Zen archery as follows:

---

phenomenon wherever it occurs. *Spiritus ubi vult spirat; The wind bloweth where it listeth* (John 3:8). Indeed, there are much greater differences between the various religions (which are obviously subject to social, cultural, historical, and even racial differences) than there is between their mysticisms — religions tend towards "convergence" in their mysticisms — and the reasons for this are similar to the reasons for the relative agreement on "spiritual anthropology": that man in himself is everywhere the same, and that the Spirit is everywhere one.

44. William James, *The Varieties of Religious Experience* (Cambridge, Mass.: Harvard University Press, 1985), 380–81.

By archery . . . the Japanese does not understand a sport but, strange as this may sound at first, a religious ritual. And consequently, by the "art" of archery he does not mean the ability of the sportsman, which can be con-trolled, more or less, by bodily exercises, but an ability whose origin is to be sought in spiritual exercises and whose aim consists in hitting a spiritual goal. . . . It is not true to say that the traditional technique of archery, since it is no longer of importance in fighting, has turned into a pleasant pastime and thereby been rendered innocuous. The "Great Doctrine" of archery tells us something very different. According to it, archery is still a matter of life and death to the extent that it is a con-test of the archer with himself; and this kind of contest is not a paltry substitute . . . [for martial contests with "outward" opponents].[45]

For them [the Japanese Zen Masters] the contest consists in the archer aiming at himself — and yet not at himself, in hitting himself — and yet not himself, and thus becoming simultaneously the aimer and the aim, the hitter and the hit. . . . Bow and arrow are only a pretext for something that could just as well happen without them, only a way to the goal, not the goal itself, only aids for the last decisive leap.[46]

Now it is well known that after "the last decisive leap" expert Zen archers can hit a bull's-eye with their eyes closed, and, as has just been evinced, Zen archery has as the ultimate goal the same "spiritual dissolution" of the differences between subject, object,

45. Eugen Herrigel, *Zen in the Art of Archery*, trans. R. F. C. Hull (New York: Vintage Books, 1971), 14–15.
46. Ibid., 16–18.

and union that is the hallmark of all mystic attainment unto the Heart and the Spirit, as already mentioned. How, since Zen archery is a spiritual activity, is this mastery of the physical art achieved, and, conversely, how exactly — and by what method — does archery achieve the ends and goal of the mystic quest? The usual spiritual techniques involved in religions in general are: teaching correct doctrine, doing good deeds (to establish the virtues in the soul), avoiding sins and vices (to eliminate the faults or blemishes of the ego), and *Oratio et Jejunium* — prayer and fasting — which address and discipline the main faculties of the soul and the body respectively, and bestow upon the person the incalculable blessings of Divine Grace. The usual spiritual techniques involved in mysticism specifically are (in addition to the spiritual exercises used in exoteric religion as just mentioned): learning correct metaphysics and practicing on principle unceasing invocation — *pray without ceasing*, as St. Paul said (1 Thessalonians 5:17) — of the Divine Names, along with (active) meditation and (passive) contemplation of and upon them, under spiritual supervision, and after ritual initiation. All of these things together eventually serve to awaken the Heart and the Spirit within man. Clearly in Zen archery there is none of the above, least of all any concretely delineated doctrine or metaphysic,[47] so how does it achieve its mystic ends? Herrigel takes us through the spiritual lessons he learnt during the course of ordinary archery practice as follows:

47. [T]he Japanese method of instruction seeks to inculcate. Practice, repetition and repetition of the repeated with ever increasing intensity are its distinctive features for long stretches of the way. At least this is true of all traditional arts. Demonstration, example; intuition, imitation — that is the fundamental relationship of instructor to pupil . . . (Eugen Herrigel, *Zen in the Art of Archery*, trans. R. F. C. Hull, 58).

In other words, no doctrine *per se* is taught in Zen Buddhism, and whatever is learned is learned by on-the-ground demonstration, experience and practice.

(1) "The right art," cried the Master, "is purposeless, aimless! The more obstinately you try to learn how to shoot for the sake of hitting the goal the less you succeed in the one and the further the other will recede. What stands in your way is that you have a much too willful will. You think that what you do not do yourself does not happen." . . . " What must I do, then?" I asked thoughtfully. "You must learn to wait properly." "And how does one learn that?" "By letting go of yourself, leaving yourself and everything of yours behind you so decisively that nothing more is left of you but a purposeless tension [when you draw the bow]."[48]

(2) "When you come to the lessons in the future" he [the Master] warned us, "you must collect yourselves on your way here. Focus your minds on what happens in the practice-hall. Walk past everything without noticing it, as if there were only one thing in the world that is important and real, and that is archery!"[49]

(3) The initial step along the road had already been taken. It had led to a loosening of the body, without which the bow cannot be drawn. If the shot is to be loosed right, the physical loosening must now be continual in a mental and spiritual loosening, so as to make the mind not only agile, but free: agile because of its freedom, and free because of its original agility; and this original agility is essentially different from everything that is usually understood by mental agility. Thus between these two states of bodily relaxedness on the one hand and

48. Ibid., 46–47.
49. Ibid., 50–51.

spiritual freedom on the other there is a difference of level which cannot be overcome by breath-control [when drawing the bow] alone, but only by withdrawing from all attachments whatsoever, by becoming utterly egoless so that the soul, sunk within itself, stands in the plenitude of its nameless origin.[50]

(4) The demand that the door of the senses be closed is not met by turning energetically away from the sensible world, but rather by a readiness to yield without resistance. In order that this actionless activity may be accomplished instinctively, the soul needs an inner hold, and it wins it by concentrating on breathing. This is performed consciously and a conscientiousness that borders on the pedantic. The breathing in, like the breathing out, is practiced again and again by itself with the utmost care. One does not have to wait long for results.[51]

(5) This exquisite state of unconcerned immersion in oneself is not, unfortunately, of long duration. It is liable to be disturbed from inside. As though sprung from nowhere, moods, feelings, desires, worries and even thoughts incontinently rise up, in a meaningless jumble, and the more far-fetched and preposterous they are, and the less they have to do with that on which one has fixed one's consciousness, the more tenaciously they hang on. . . . The only successful way of rendering this disturbance inoperative is to keep breathing quietly and unconcernedly, to enter into friendly relations with whatever appears on the scene, to accustom oneself to it, to look at it equably and at last grow weary of looking.

50. Ibid., 51–52.
51. Ibid., 52.

. . . [If you are able to resist falling asleep] the soul is brought to the point where it vibrates of itself in itself. . . . This state, in which nothing definite is thought, planned, striven for, desired or expected, which aims in no particular direction . . . this state, which is at bottom purposeless and egoless, was called by the Master truly "spiritual." It is in fact charged with spiritual awareness and is therefore also called "right presence of mind."[52]

(6) During these weeks and months I passed through the hardest schooling of my life, and though the discipline was not always easy for me to accept, I gradually came to see how much I was indebted to it. It destroyed the last traces of any preoccupations with myself and the fluctuations of my mood.[53]

It was mentioned earlier that religious techniques work by addressing themselves to (and encompassing) all the various faculties of the soul and the body, and that mystical techniques work by addressing themselves to (and awakening) the Heart and the Spirit. It is evident in all the passages just quoted that Zen archery employs different spiritual techniques to fulfill in fact exactly the same goals. The first passage, though ostensibly referring to "the will," refers not so much to the will as such, but to the will as directed by the ego, and therein the Master seeks not only to weaken the ego, but also to "undo" concentration of the will directed toward an "antispiritual" end. Conversely, in the second passage, the will having been "relaxed" away from its egotistic "end," is now "refocused" and "reconcentrated" toward a "spiritual end," along with the intelligence and sentiment, and the "animal" soul is upbraided by not being allowed to wallow in its own passivity and being forced to be

52. Ibid., 53–55.
53. Ibid., 85.

vigilant in spiritual purpose. In the third passage, the archer learns how to divest his / her soul of all interference from both the "ego" and the "id" alike at any given moment, and in the fourth passage the archer learns to use breathing to divest his / her soul from all interference from the body. In the fifth passage the author describes the state of the "pure soul" when fully in possession of itself and ignoring the interference from the natural passivity and laziness of the soul and the body, and thus when it is potentially most recep- tive to the Heart. Finally, in the sixth passage the author alludes to the process of the virtues taking permanent root in the soul such that the temporary "state" mentioned in the previous passage can become a permanent "station," as with mystic quests in other reli- gions. Nor should there be any doubt as to the ultimate efficacy of these methods, for Herrigel makes their spiritual results — and thus genuineness[54] of Zen archery as a form of mysticism — quite clear (that is, in so far as these "results" are not completely ineffable)[55]:

> [A]ll right doing is accomplished only in a state of true selflessness, in which the doer cannot be present any longer as "himself." Only the spirit is present, a kind of awareness which shows no trace of egohood and for that reason ranges without limit through all the distances and depths, with "eyes that hear and with ears that see."[56]

> To be free from the fear of death does not mean pretend- ing to oneself, in one's good hours, that one will not

54. Jesus (ﷺ) said (Matthew 7:16): *Ye shall know them by their fruits.*

55. No reasonable person would expect a Zen adept to do more than hint at the experiences which have liberated and changed him, or to attempt to describe the unimaginable and ineffable "Truth" by which he now lives. In this respect Zen is akin to pure introspective mysticism. Unless we enter into mystic experiences by direct participation, we remain outside, turn and twist as we may. (Herrigel, *Zen in the Art of Archery*, 20.)

56. Ibid., 64.

tremble in the face of death, and that there is nothing to fear. Rather, he who masters both life and death is free from fear of any kind to the extent that he is no longer capable of experiencing what fear feels like. Those who do not know the power of rigorous and protracted meditation cannot judge of the self-conquests it makes possible.[57]

Every Master who practices an art moulded by Zen is like a flash of lightning from the cloud of all-encompassing Truth. This Truth is present in the free movement of his spirit, and he meets it again, in "It," as his own original and nameless essence. He meets this essence over and over again, so that the Truth assumes for him — and for others through him — a thousand shapes and forms.

In spite of the unexampled discipline to which he has patiently and humbly subjected he is still a long way from being so permeated and irradiated by Zen that he is sustained by it in everything he does, so that his life knows only good hours. The supreme freedom has still not become a necessity for him.

If he is irresistibly driven toward this goal, he must set out on his way again, take the road to the artless art. He must dare to leap into the Origin, so as to live by the Truth and in the Truth, like one who has become one with it. He must become a pupil again, a beginner; conquer the last and steepest stretch of the way, undergo new transformations. If he survives its perils, then his destiny is fulfilled: face to face he beholds the unbroken Truth, the Truth beyond all truths, the formless Origin of origins, the Void which is the All, is absorbed into it and from it emerges reborn.[58]

57. Ibid., 103–4.
58. Ibid., 106–7.

Presumably the first two passages and the first paragraph of the last passage refer to the "stage" or "spiritual experience" of the Heart, whereas the last paragraph of the third passage, with its "new transformations" and its "face to face behold[ing of] the unbroken Truth" refers to the Spirit and to the "journey in the Spirit." It will also be noted that although the Zen rites had hitherto almost assiduously avoided all mention of theology or doctrine, concentrating instead on method and virtue, in these advanced spiritual stages it became unavoidable to mention the [Divine] Truth[59] by Name, for what is spiritual attainment other than knowledge of God, knowledge of the Truth?

Thus there can be no doubt as to the ultimate mystic nature or efficacy of the practice of archery in Zen Buddhism. Moreover, Herrigel also points out that Zen mysticism is the basis of other Japanese sports and arts:

[T]he Japanese arts go back for their inner form to a common root, namely Buddhism. This is as true of the art of archery as of ink painting, of the art of the theatre no less than the tea ceremony, the art of flower arrangement, and swordsmanship. All of them presuppose a spiritual attitude and each cultivates it in its own way — an attitude which, in its most exalted form, is characteristic of Buddhism and determines the nature of the priestly type of man. I do not mean Buddhism in the ordinary sense, nor am I concerned here with the decidedly speculative form of Buddhism . . . I mean Dhyana Buddhism, which is known in Japan as "Zen" and is not speculation at all but immediate experience of what, as the bottomless

59. It will be noticed that in Islam *Al-Haqq*, "the Truth," is one of the Divine Names, and that among the "ninety-nine" Names of God, there are near-synonyms for "the Origin," "the All," and "the Void."

ground of Being, cannot be apprehended by rational means, and cannot be conceived [as a purely mental construct] or interpreted even after the most unequivocal and incontestable experiences: one knows it by not knowing it.[60]

Herrigel even goes so far as to give details concerning several of these arts and sports, but it will suffice here to quote only his insights on swordsmanship:

Perfection in the art of swordsmanship is reached, according to Takuan [a Master swordsman], when the heart is troubled by no more thought of I and You, of the opponent and his sword, of one's own sword and how to yield it — no more thought even of life and death. "All is emptiness: your own self, the flashing sword, and the arms that wield it. Even the thought of emptiness is no longer." From this absolute emptiness, states Taukan, "comes the most wondrous unfoldment of doing."[61]

Thus far in our discussion of mysticism in sports we have restricted ourselves to quoting mainly from Eugen Herrigel and discussing mainly sports associated with Zen Buddhist mysticism. Obviously, however, there are many sports originating in mystic rites in other religions. Aside from archery[62] and, as hinted at earlier, the mystic undertones to wrestling, the Oriental martial arts, and chess (see Appendix A), it remains only to be said that the

61. Ibid., 101.
62. In addition to that in Zen Buddhism, the symbolism and practice of archery in the worlds of Ancient Egypt, Iraq, Greece (witness the test of stringing Odysseus's bow and shooting it through twelve Cretan double axes at the end of The Odyssey), and, especially, India (witness The Mahabharata) are also well known. What is not so well known, however, is the rich tradition of archery, and even sacred archery in the Islamic world. At the beginning of the

most famous instance of this is obviously Yoga in Hindu mysti-cism.[63] This is clearly evinced in the following passage from one of the texts held sacred in Hinduism:

> Day after day, let the Yogi practise the harmony of the soul: in a secret place, in deep solitude, master of his

---

nineteenth century, Mustafa Kani wrote a treatise, *Telkhis Rasail al-Rumat*, for Sultan Mahmoud II (one of the greatest patrons of archery, and in particular of the Ottoman archer's guild) in which he cited forty *ahadith* (sayings of the Prophet [ﷺ]) about archery, and wherein he definitively summarized Islamic teachings on the subject. Thus it transpires that the bow represents the very Majesty of God, and that the first bow was given to Adam by the Archangel Gabriel (ﷺ) to protect his crops from birds (birds here having the spiritual symbolism as in the Parable of the Sower). Moreover, the Prophet Abraham was the first to "receive" a composite bow, and he and his elder son the Prophet Ismail (ﷺ — this being, incidentally, another indication of the antediluvian origin of sports) were both celebrated archers. Finally, it is said that the Prophet Muhammad himself (ﷺ) practiced archery, and that his cousin and companion, the famous general Sa'ad bin Abi Waqqas, became the archetypal model for the Muslim archer / saint.

All this was possible only because archery itself inherently comprises (and hence can potentially actualize) the symbolism of "intellection," of spiritual "penetration," and above all of the release of the spirit from the soul, i.e., of the mystical, spiritual states. Moreover, every part of a bow and arrow translates directly into a "golden" or "alchemical" symbolism, and there is even a "con-templative sexual" symbolism in archery involved in the bending of the tips of the bow. In short, archery was everywhere as a religious practice because, beyond its uses for worldly power, it is inherently a mirror of the highest spiri-tual activity of which man is capable.

63. Dancing, which according to our definition of sport at the beginning of the essay qualifies as a "sport," does of course also have mystic undertones — if not mystic origins — in many religions, notably in Hinduism, in the Native American religions, and in Islamic mysticism or "sufism." Moreover, in these mystic dances, rhythm, movement, and breathing all assume precise spiritual symbolism — as does the state of exhaustion at the end of the dance — which can serve to induce the loftiest mystic states. See Martin Lings, *A Sufi Saint of the Twentieth Century*, 95–97.

mind, hoping for nothing. Let him find a place that is pure and a seat that is restful, neither too high nor too low, with sacred grass and a skin and a cloth thereupon. On that seat let him rest and practice Yoga for the purification of the soul: with the life of the body and mind in peace; his soul in silence before the One. With upright body, head, and neck, and which rest still and move not; with inner gaze which is not restless but rests still between the eyebrows; with soul in peace, and all fear gone, and strong in the vow of holiness, let him rest his mind in harmony. . . ."[64]

64. *The Bhagavad Gita*, trans. Juan Mascaro (New York: Viking Press, 1983), 6, 10–14.

(IV) GENERAL NATURE OF SPORTS

OBVIOUSLY, HOWEVER, IT could not be said that the majority of sports are still part of formal religion, let alone mysticism, and even those sports that survive relatively intact (such as martial arts, as already mentioned) from their original religious forms are by intention anything but sacred.[65] On the other hand, the majority of sports practiced today, because of their spiritual origins, are still on principle *edifying and wholesome* in nature and thus *beneficial to both body and soul* of those who practice them. We say "the majority" because it seems to us that certain "sports" (if they can indeed be legitimately regarded as such) — such as synchronized swimming, blood-sports,[66] professional wrestling, and body-building[67] — have

---

65. As will later be seen, sports nowadays take on the proportions, zeal, and trappings of cults — as with the giant, sopish, global-village festivities that accompany the Olympic Games — but this has nothing to do with "sacredness" as such and is "religious" *only* in the sense that great human devotion is involved.

66. In Islam, although it is licit to kill (certain) animals in order to eat them, the Prophet (ﷺ) cursed anyone who takes anything possessing life as a target (according to both Bukhari and Muslim) and forbade making animals fight each other (according to Abu Dawud and Al-Tirmidhi).

67. Our objections to body-building, which has become quite a widespread and popular activity in our days, are directed at the vanity, arrogance, and spirit of exhibitionism it inherently induces, and at the fact that the bodies it manufactures (whilst by normal standards obviously extremely strong) are designed *a priori* neither for strength (like power lifters) nor endurance (like track athletes) — much less for flexibility or physical fitness — but sheerly for size and appearance. Thus, body-builders are not *necessarily* healthy (even when they do not take steroids), are highly prone to injury, are badly suited for any real physical tasks, and, as if all this were not bad enough, inherently come to have the superficial mentality of believing that what counts is show and appearance, which obviously is the furthest possible thing from truth and virtue. Needless to

little intrinsic meaning and are actually detrimental to the soul if not to the body and to physical health or well-being.

Precisely how, then, are the majority of sports *"edifying and wholesome* in nature and thus potentially *beneficial to both body and soul"*? First, as regards the "soul," it is still true that despite the lack of awareness of the true meaning of certain sports by even their most expert practitioners, their very forms and motions, when relativily intact, retain in themselves — and confer upon all who practice or witness them — considerable "subconscious value," due to their beauty, their nobility of content and their spiritually correct symbolism. Moreover, they obviously also retain a "dormant potential" which can at any time be re-awakened:

> The symbolic content of an art is originally bound up with its practical function, but is not necessarily lost when under changed conditions the art is no longer practiced of necessity but as a game or sport; and even when such a sport has become completely secularized and has become for the profane a mere recreation or amusement, it is still possible for whoever possesses the requisite knowledge of traditional symbolism to complete this physical participation in the sport, or enjoyment of it as a spectacle, by an understanding of its forgotten significance, and so restore, for himself at least, the "polar balance of physical and metaphysical" that is characteristic of all traditional cultures.[68]

Second, even the practice of ordinary sports inherently instills and teaches some virtue if not all of the possible virtues to

---

say, however, we are the last to object to a balanced and healthy regimen of weight training in conjunction with other sports, cardiovascular exercise, and, above all, physical modesty.

68. A. K. Coomarswamy, *What Is Civilisation?*, 135.

man.[69] One could say that the *discipline* intrinsic to the mastery of any sport teaches sacrifice, patience, self-control, temperance, and detachment. Similarly, one could say that the *effort* required teaches strength, will-power, energy, positive activity, and decisiveness. Equally, the *sportsmanship* necessary to be a sports competitor means learning charity, generosity, friendship, courtesy, and even nobility.[70] Then, *team-work* and the inevitable experience of occasionally losing teach the virtues of humility and contentment, and thus also the art of keeping one's morale high. The element of *strategy* in sports exercises the intelligence and requires objectivity. Finally, the necessity of proper *organization* requires concentration, recollectedness, unity, and self-domination. In short, discipline and effort engage the virtues associated with volition in its static and dynamic modes respectively; sportsmanship and team-work engage the virtues associated with sentiment in its active and passive modes respectively; and strategy and organization engage the intelligence in its analytic and synthetic modes respectively. Moreover, since these three "dimensions" — will, sentiment and intelligence — and the virtues associated with them are the three

---

69. As perhaps is already clear, this is different — or rather on a lower "level" — from the action of mysticism in sports, because mysticism pertains, strictly speaking, to the Spirit, and the virtues pertain to the soul, albeit that the perfection of the virtues of the soul leads to (and in fact is the necessary prerequisite of) the awakening of the Spirit.

70. Benjamin Franklin, in his delightful essay on "The Morals of Chess," *The Works of Benjamin Franklin* (Cincinnati: U. P. James, 1838) says the following:

> You must not, when you have gained a victory, use any triumphing or insulting expression, nor show too much pleasure; but endeavor to console your adversary, and make him less dissatisfied with himself by every kind and civil expression, that may be used with truth; such as: "You understand the game better than I, but you are a little inattentive"; or "You play too fast"; or "You had the best of the game but something happened to divert your thoughts."

primary faculties of the human soul (as explained in the previous section), it can easily be seen how sports engage, or can engage, the whole of man.

There are also three or four other kinds of experience inherent in sports which are — or can be — invaluable to the soul, and to its general well-being or "virtue." First and most obviously, there is the general fact and symbolism of *playing* which — bearing in mind all the different kinds of elements mentioned above and bearing in mind the various rules that are part of each and every different sport — inherently reflect the moral quest of man and therefore the human condition as such. After all, according to all genuine tradition and all true religion, what counts in life is not what one has achieved in a worldly sense (i.e., whether one has won the "game" or not) but *how* one has "played the game," what "character" one has shown and how one has followed the (moral) rules.[71] Thus the Prophet (ﷺ) said: *Verily acts are [accomplished] in the intention [behind them], and every person will get what they intended.*[72] In short, the mere activity of playing sports can and should teach a contemplative person that it is the moral content of life that matters above all, and not worldly or financial achievements. Virtue is its own reward, and it is, moreover, a permanent and eternal victory, since the soul is immortal. Without virtue a game, even a game won, is just a game, and this applies as much to the game of worldly success as to sports.

However, if a game won is not to be regarded as the goal or even the most important aspect of sports, nevertheless, the

---

71. This is also the reason why the Prophet (ﷺ) called the greater Holy War (*Al-Jihad Al-Akbar*) "the war against the [evils of the] soul" and the lesser Holy War (*Al-Jihad Al-Asghar*) the "physical" war to defend the community or *Umma* of Islam.

72. Bukhari, *Sahih* Vol. 1, *Kitab Al-Iman*, ch. 42.

experience of winning in sports is still capable of being of immense worth to the sportsperson. For *winning* itself demands — *de jure* if not *de facto* (for some victories come too easy, *really*) — doing one's best, and thus implies total commitment to something, which is a great, and even an indispensable, virtue since there is no moral (let alone spiritual) life without determination and unity of purpose. Indeed, *Itqan* ("mastery" or right action, which stems from total commitment) is considered as the fourth of the five cardinal qualities for Muslims after *Islam* (submission to God; right doctrine); *Iman* (faith; right belief); and *Ihsan* (virtue; right worship), and before *Ikhlas* (sincerity; right being). Moreover, "mastery" is in itself the first step — and thus the *sine qua non* — toward self-mastery, which is "spiritual victory" over the vices and evil of one's own ego, the reward for which is nothing other than Heaven. This also explains why, *really*, it is better to play well and lose than play badly and win.

There is yet another point to consider and this is the actual "spiritual symbolism" of winning as such. Here, the opponent whom one defeats symbolizes oneself, or rather the "self" which one has to transcend. Being able to see this inherently presupposes a considerable act of both insight and charity, for it requires the ability to go beyond the natural myopia of subjectivity, of the "I" which believes that it is the only "I." "Looking back" objectively to see one's "true self" from the point of view of "another" requires an even greater movement "outside" of oneself, for it evidently means actually putting oneself fully in one's (defeated) opponent's shoes for a moment:

> To "become the enemy" means to think yourself into the enemy's position. In the world people tend to think of a robber trapped in a house as a fortified enemy. However, if we think of "becoming the enemy," we feel that the whole world is against us and that there is no escape. He

THE SACRED ORIGIN OF SPORTS AND CULTURE

who is shut inside is a pheasant. He who enters to arrest
is a hawk. You must appreciate this. [73]

In fact, fully appreciating the above also leads to the Second
Commandment — the ability to *love thy neighbor as thyself*[74] — for
understanding someone cannot but naturally bring empathy, if
not sympathy, for that person. Conversely, not appreciating the
above means there is nothing to be learned from one's own actions
— and so nothing to be gained from the opponent's defeat —
making all victory pyrrhic. And if the inherent detachment and
benevolence of this complex mirror-play seems to obfuscate the
obvious and natural joys of winning, it should be borne in mind
that he who dominates himself in winning has *ipso facto*, dominated not just one opponent or two, but the whole world. "He
who overcomes others is strong; he who overcomes himself is
mighty."[75] Furthermore, the dividend of this mightiness is nothing
other than true happiness, for through self-domination one puts
oneself beyond being affected by anything or anyone. It is in precisely this sense that the Prophet said: *All is well with the faithful,
whatever the circumstances.*[76]

All the above pertains to the potential and spiritual moral
benefits of the experience of winning. What remains to be said is
obviously that winning also has a certain value for the sports competitor when he (or she) is representing his or her country, club,
or region, but only on condition that victory represents an act of
excellence and above all a sacrifice dedicated to a given group
which itself represents a certain ideal which, even if it is not

73. Miyamoto Musachi, *A Book of Five Rings*, trans. Victor Harris (Boston:
Shambhala, 1994), 75.

74. Matthew 22:39.

75 Lao Tzu, *Tao Te Ching*, 33, trans. Stephen Mitchell (New York: Harper
and Row, 1988), 33.

76. Al-Nasa'i, *Sunan*, vol. 21, 13.

spiritual, is nevertheless morally praiseworthy, and is inclusive of all that wish to share in it and appreciate it. Indeed, competition must never by design parochially exclude a given set of people or be taken to prove the superiority or inferiority of X or Y (as in the Berlin Olympic Games before the Second World War where German victory was supposed to show the superiority of the "Aryan race" over all others) except in that sport itself and on that particular occasion only. In short, professional and international sports competition as such have value as *communal sacrifice* only in so far as the event takes place in a spirit of bringing different people together in friendship, mutual respect, and cooperation, such that the sportsperson can give his or her all *for* someone or something,[77] and not *against* someone or something *per se*. This in fact was the original and "real" idea behind the Olympic Games, and the fact that exactly the opposite is more usually the case in the modern world, even in the Olympics, is irrelevant to the principle of the matter.

Another type of morally constructive experience inherent in sports which will be mentioned here is the phenomenon of the *spectacle* of sports and the *beauty* it can potentially produce. Of course, one does not normally nowadays think of associating sports with beauty, because on the one hand the modern world would have us think that beauty is a subjective fiction and that it is synonymous with taste, and on the other hand the modern world tries to drown us in the evidently undeniable and objective beauty of

---

77. We do not mean this in a humanistic — and therefore secular — sense. In all religions service to the community, to *love thy neighbour as thyself* (Leviticus 19:18, Matthew 19:19, and so on) is a moral obligation first because charity and compassion are essential virtues, and second because our neighbor is made in God's *own image* (Genesis 1:27), as we ourselves are. Furthermore, in certain religions such as Confucianism and Shintoism the community itself takes on a directly sacred meaning.

the human body. However, there is nevertheless potentially a real beauty in sports that everyone who watches consciously or unconsciously looks out for and hopes to see. This can come in the grace of actions performed in sports, in the skills behind them, in their technical correctness, in the beauty of their forms and gestures and even in the virtue manifested by the competitors themselves. In fact, there is a whole category of modern sports won through beauty and technical correctness, such as gymnastics, ice-skating, diving, and so on. The ones, however, where beauty is the most real are naturally the older ones such as the martial arts, wherein there are ritual patterns (*katas* or *poomses*) which are judged for their "beauty and skill." However, in these cases the beauty in question does not merely consist of "natural beauty," as with the sports just mentioned, but rather is — at least by intent and originally — the embodiment of certain "mythological dramas" which play out the rhythms of nature, and hence the Divine Qualities within and behind them.

There are also categories of sports — such as horse-riding, fencing, archery, and (amateur) wrestling — in which beauty as such does not count toward winning the sport, but is nevertheless what makes the sport worth watching. The ball-games (such as baseball, soccer, cricket, American football, rugby, basketball, tennis, golf, and so on), which are by far the most popular kind of sport in the modern world, and which for that reason are veritable "billion dollar industries," can be said to afford certain undeniable displays of skill, but have nothing like the grace inherent in any of the other, already-mentioned sports. It is, however, difficult to say this to people nowadays — bewitched as they are by the confrontational and personal qualities of these sports and by their meaningless technicalities — but from a traditional philosophical point of view the aesthetic value of ball games as such is not particularly high.

Finally, the last component of sports beneficial to the soul that we will mention here is doubtlessly the most obvious. It is the legitimate and even necessary aspect of *relaxation* that all real sports, even the seemingly most meaningless, affords spectators and players alike. Relaxation is in fact as necessary to the soul as it is to the body — which is traditionally held to be the corporeal image of the soul and which is subject to the same "rhythms" of expansion and contraction, of tension and ease, as the soul — for the soul by its own nature cannot endure indefinite tension without "cracking" and cannot be constantly only doing its duties, praying, and working. In this lower world, the soul needs "expansion" to counteract the pressure of "contraction," just as the body needs to exhale after it inhales. Indeed, a proper balance of work and relaxation is the way to strengthen the soul's capacity and endurance for work, just as a proper balance of physical exercise and rest makes the body stronger and fitter. Thus one of the companions of the Prophet (ﷺ), Abu al-Darda, explained: *I entertain my heart with something trivial in order to make it stronger in the service of the truth.*[78]

Of course, it need hardly be said that in the modern world "the pursuit of happiness" is held to be a goal in life — and perhaps even *the* goal of life — and therefore does not need the justification of being "in the service of the truth" in the minds of many people (and thus obviously neither do sports simply on the grounds that they licitly make people happy). What is not known, however, is that even in the most ascetic and austere of traditional cultures, happiness (albeit one sprinkled with sobriety) is a legitimate and even commendable goal simply because it is necessary to human nature:

> *Do not abandon yourself to grief or go out of your way to distress yourself. A merry heart keeps a person alive, and joy*

---

78. Quoted from Yousif al-Qaradawi, *The Lawful and the Prohibited in Islam* (Indianapolis: American Trust Publications, 1980), 292.

lengthens the span of days. Indulge yourself, take comfort, and
banish grief far from you; for grief has been the death of many
and no advantage ever came of it. Envy and anger shorten life,
and anxiety brings premature old age. He who has a light heart
[has] a good appetite and enjoys the food he eats.[79]

AT THIS POINT the obvious question arises — and indeed it is,
metaphysically speaking, the most crucial in the whole issue of
sports — as to *why* it is in the nature of man, especially given that
he is *made in the image of God* (Genesis1:27), to enjoy and naturally benefit from sports? After all, we know that the Divine
Nature is the Absolute, and that it is the Truth, and since this
obviously is the furthest possible thing from the levity and jest of
sports, how then could there also be in this Nature the
Archetype of sports? As the Qur'an says (16:3): *He hath created*
the heavens and earth with Truth. . . . The answer to this is that if,
in one respect, the world was created *with truth* (and was so of
necessity because every creation cannot but reflect its Creator
even if only partially or indirectly), this nevertheless does not
exclude its being in another respect a "movement away" from the
Absolute Truth of God Himself, so that in fact the very movement of "emanation" inherent in manifestation itself is a kind of
"sport" for God, in the sense that nothing that goes on in it can
take away from — or add to — His own Nature, and thus His
Omnipotence, His Omniscience, and His Absolute Freedom.
Thus the Prophet (ﷺ) said: *If the world were equal to [the worth*
of] the wing of a gnat to God, He would not have given a single sin-
ner [even] a drink of water.[80] In other words — and this point is a

79. Ecclesiastes 30:21–27.
80. Al-Tirmidhi, *Sunan, Kitab Al-Zuhd*, 13.

logical dialectic which is very easy to misunderstand — although there is a great, providential purpose in creation as such and in the particular creation of which we are a part, nevertheless God in Himself remains Absolutely transcendent of everything, because in the first place nothing can affect His Immutability, and in the second place everything that has truth or reality in creation comes from the Divine and is merely its manifestation. In short, as with sports in their original forms, the world is an ambiguous tapestry of truth and illusion, jest and reality, which can lead, through prayer, to God. Thus the Qur'an says (21:16): *We created not the heaven and the earth and all that is between them in play,* but also says (57:20): *Know that the life of this world is only play, and idle talk, and pageantry, and boasting among you, and rivalry in respect of wealth and children.* . . . The ultimate archetype of sports is thus creation itself, and sports are to man in a sense what creation is to God. This is their ultimate secret and their most profound symbolism, and this is the deepest reason why they were originally religious rites.[81]

Finally in this section, having mentioned all the possible benefits of sports to the soul, it is perhaps a truism to say that they are of immeasurable benefit to the body as well, by keeping it healthy and vigorous throughout life, and by preventing it from falling into inactivity and physical deterioration. In fact, if there is one point about which modern medicine is unanimous it is that nothing is better for long-term health than a regular and balanced regimen of physical exercise and sports. Moreover, bodily health is the most important

---

81. We hesitated to mention this rather metaphysical and esoteric point in a section of the essay that otherwise contains some fairly mundane ideas and facts, but it seemed to us that not to mention it would be to miss the deepest symbolism of sports. Furthermore, since it is in the nature of sport itself, as we have hopefully already explained, to span the range from "the sublime to the ridiculous," then a proper exposition of the subject cannot but do the same.

thing in life after the "health of the soul,"[82] for without bodily health nothing in life is either pleasurable or possible. As Juvenal said: *"Orandum est ut sit mens sana in corpore sano"* ("You should pray for a healthy mind in a healthy body").

Moreover, the benefits of physical health do not extend merely to the body, but also to the soul itself, and this is yet another way in which sports benefit it. Of course we know that there are a great many people nowadays who do not believe in the existence of the soul and many who have no idea what it is (see section iii), but from the point of view of traditional philosophy what is more dangerous, intellectually speaking, is the idea — first made prevalent by Descartes and more or less ubiquitous today — that the soul and body comprise a sharp separation or "dualism" that is moreover split asunder at death. In fact, as already discussed, the soul and the body are intimately connected such that it is in effect difficult to say where the one ends and the other begins, and this is why the health of the body portends positively for the health of the soul. The very word "disease" comes from this idea — or rather, from its negation — for "dis"-"ease" of the mind brings "disease" of the body, and indeed modern medicine now recognizes the major role of what it calls "stress" (which is nothing other than mental and emotional "disease") in everything from migraines and shingles to cancer and heart attacks.

We may thus conclude that even when they seem to be benefiting the body, sports can benefit the soul as well (and vice versa) and thus that they are, just as we have already stated, thoroughly and inherently both *edifying and wholesome*, beneficial as

---

82. The "health of the soul" is faith and virtue and these are nothing less than the very object of life and of human existence. God says in the Qur'an (51:56): *I created the jinn and humankind only that they might worship Me . . .*, and what is worship other than faith and virtue?

much to the soul as to the body, even when not consciously undertaken in their original, spiritual forms. It is no doubt with this in mind that the Prophet (ﷺ) said, quite simply: *Practice archery; that is good for you.*83

83. Reported by Al-Bazzar and by Al-Tabarani on good authority.

(v) SPORTS IN THE MODERN WORLD

IN THE PREVIOUS three parts of this essay we have discussed how sports have spiritual origins and how they are in principle beneficial in nature to body and soul. In this part of the essay we aim to discuss the abuses of sports in the modern world, bearing in mind *a priori* that these abuses in no wise change all that has previously been said about sports or reflect upon their inherent nature and worth, any more than transgressions reflect upon the religions in whose name they are committed, or than a crime committed in someone's name who in reality has no knowledge of it condemns the latter before the law. In other words, it must be borne in mind throughout this section that the abuse of sports in the modern world speaks negatively of the modern world first and foremost, and not necessarily negatively of sports themselves.

Having said this, the first criticism that must be made of sports in our day is the simple point, already mentioned, that despite all of the enthusiasm surrounding them today there exists little, if any, understanding of their real worth and sacerdotal origins; i.e., of all that we have just said about them. Of course, we said at the onset that a doctrinal understanding of the subject was in no wise necessary for the benefits to be reaped from their practice provided that a positive attitude is maintained — and this is true — but it is precisely the case that having some measure of conceptual understanding of their true nature and origin helps to maintain a "positive attitude" in the first place, if it does not enrich the experience altogether.

Indeed, sports have now become completely "autotelic" and are practiced without reference to moral or physical edification —

that is, they purport to have their own *raison d'être* within themselves or rather, not to need a *raison d'être* at all — and the question of their being in the service of a "higher purpose," even as training for war or for martial exercises, does not even arise. The situation is akin to that of art in the modern world which now exists independently of — and even in opposition to — the notions of truth and beauty which were formerly their *sine qua non*. Art for art's sake and sport for sport's sake, as if shadows did not need anything to cast them or as if life could be endless jest and heedlessness and at the same time be meaningful. Clearly, this view of sports as "autotelic," while apparently promoting their practice and granting them the status of "independence," greatly impoverishes their potential benefits, despite what their modern promoters might say.

The next criticism that must be made of sports today is also obvious: it is simply that there is just too much of them. There is not only too much of them played, there are too many kinds of them (often with negligible differences between them), and too much time, energy, and money are wasted upon playing them, watching them, discussing them, and thinking about them, especially given the previous point! After all, even breathing too much oxygen will lead to a headache, and even drinking too much water will lead to an upset stomach. An uncannily prophetic text,[84] first published in 1927, complains:

> [T]he Anglo-Saxon passion for "sport" gains more and more ground every day; the ideal of the modern world is

84 René Guénon, *The Crisis of the Modern World* (trans. M. Pallis and R. Nicholson), 91–92. It is perhaps not without meaning that in the world-famous O. J. Simpson double murder trial of 1994–95 — whose very fame itself speaks realms about the status of sports heroes in the modern world — the prosecution, despite the heinousness of the alleged crime, did not even demand the death penalty, because, as the newspapers said: 'Americans simply will not send O. J. Simpson [an American football legend] to the electric chair, no matter what crime.'

113

the "human animal" who has developed his muscular strength to the utmost; its heroes are the athletes, should they even be brutes; it is they who awaken the popular enthusiasm and it is their exploits that command the passionate interest of the crowd.

Seventy years later, the world's media has so thoroughly adopted the cause of sports publicity — with television, the newspapers, and now even computers having their own sections on sports news — that even those completely uninterested in the subject are forced to swallow a daily dose of its on-going trivia, and this is to say nothing of the social pressures on the youth and even on adults to be conversant in this trivia, especially in industrially developed countries.

Needless to say, too much sports, especially when devoid of metaphysical undercurrents, means too much time spent "in" and "on" the body. In other words, there is a natural balance between the "time" a person may legitimately spend in the activities "of the body" and the time he or she must spend in the activities "of the soul" (to say nothing of those "of the spirit"). The amount of "time" and "concentration" that modern sports, at a competitive level, can entail cannot but upset this balance to the detriment of the soul and all the higher human faculties.

Man has a body, but he is not an animal, and mastering and transcending himself is part of his specifically human prerogative, and even is the categorical imperative of his state. Thus, man cannot sink completely into his body without becoming sub-human in certain ways.[85] This, however, is precisely the fate of those obsessed by sports for their own sake, *for where your treasure is,*

85. This is precisely the meaning of the warning of the parable of the talents (Matthew 25:14–31), that *there shall be weeping and gnashing of teeth* for he who buries his "talents."

there will your heart be also (Luke 13:34 — "heart" here means the "subtle heart," the highest part of the soul as in *Blessed are the pure in heart*, Matthew 5:8, and as already mentioned in section (iii) of this essay). One "becomes" what one loves, and if one loves the body too much, one becomes reduced to it and thus one becomes an animal.[86]

Moreover, there is an even more sinister aspect to this "descent into the body" than mere "tragic waste," and it verges on idolatry of the body and the physical senses and thus of what is associated with them par excellence:

> Today sports have become like a religion in the modern West . . . In the Islamic world the assembly of very large crowds in a public function has almost always been in relation to religion as one can see in the *Hajj* or in Muharram ceremonies of the Shi'ite world. Today, however, there are vast sport spectacles which have by and large replaced traditional religious functions. . . . There is a strain in the current lifestyle which concerns the attempt to live in the present moment indifferent to one's history and the past and immersed in instantaneous sensuous gratification and glorification. The worship of sports heroes and the continuous quest for record breaking and the domination over nature . . . reflect the attempt of the soul to immerse itself completely in immediate bodily and sensual gratification [and is *a priori* a result of] the excessive importance given to the body.[87]

---

86. Or rather, one becomes worse than an animal, for animals are innocent of sin and guilt and have every right to be what they are.

87. Seyyed Hossein Nasr, *A Young Muslim's Guide to the Modern World* (Chicago: Kazi Publications, 1997), 232–33.

There is thus in the modern world a kind of cult of form and of the body akin to the one we see manifested in later Greek and Roman art (by which time their civilizations had reached the stage of moral decline), and this cult feeds on — and is in turn fed on by — the omnipresence of sports in modern culture. This is perhaps inevitable because sports have been reduced, as explained earlier, largely to mere activities of the body, and because the body itself, *made in the image of God*, has also been robbed of its higher significance. Also, it need hardly be said that this "cult" of athleticism and of "the body perfect" is not unrelated to the mad, insatiable obsession with sex — or rather with promiscuity — which has gripped modern culture in every single realm from modern biology and psychology to fashion and cinema. Furthermore, the obsession with sports is perhaps as much a cause as a symptom of the obsession with sex, for evidently the two strengthen each other through their common focus on the body, its functions, its needs, its wants, and its performances.

Another ill of modern sports is the phenomenon of "professional sports." Professional sports ignore the fact that work and play are two different, separate human needs: they constitute a confusion that fails to take into account the separate psychological needs for earnestness in work and for levity in play — to the inevitable detriment of both — and this is to say nothing of the net social, economic, and cultural uselessness of professional athletes as such. Indeed, the social maladjustment from which professional athletes suffer even before they become too old or too injured to practice a sport is a clear symptom of this, and despite the massive preparation and publicity surrounding professional sports events, it is difficult to imagine, even at world class level, that victories in such sports (and *a fortiori* defeats) can be anything but pyrrhic for a human being in full possession of his or her intellectual, moral, and emotional faculties. One of the saving graces of the Olympics in the modern world is precisely its encouragement of amateur sports — or at least of certain amateur sports — and its retention of the standards of excellence in sports at least theoretically within the range of the amateur practitioner.

Needless to say it is professionalism in sports — coupled evidently with the lack of moral purpose, as already discussed — that has enabled commercialism so entirely to hijack the purpose and spirit of sports in the modern world, for professional athletes are financial hostages to the sports they play and it is they that are there for the convenience of those sports rather than vice versa. Indeed, professional sports are, in the modern world, an international multi-billion dollar industry that needs no single individual, and that is quite able and willing to create, out of nothing, its own cultural "icons" which in turn bring in ever-increasing revenues. In short, professional sports, its athletes and its financial entrepreneurs are dominated by two considerations and two considerations only: money and prestige, and no single individual or group of individuals ultimately matter to it or can stop it.

To make matters yet worse, this double scourge (of money and prestige) acquires a total value greater than that of the sum of its parts, because it becomes the yardstick of a whole basket of inescapable (because they are natural) subconscious or subliminal needs and motives, notably "job-satisfaction," "self-fulfillment," "self esteem," and "social productivity." In other words, money and prestige, because they measure success in sports and because sports, have become professional work, and also come to determine how professional athletes look upon themselves, the world and moral values. This is to say nothing of the spiritually detrimental effects of the undeserved money,[88] fame, and prestige that come if success is

88. In the mid-1990s champion boxers like heavyweight Mike Tyson were commanding fees of up to 30 million U.S. dollars for a single fight, and the top basketball player, Michael Jordan, was earning over 50 million dollars a year (in

attained. Thus the vices of greed and vanity start to dominate even those athletes who initially started with the most normal and legitimate psychic elements and motives for wanting to "turn professional." We do not say, of course, that all professional athletes are bound to become evil, but only that they are likely to find it increasingly difficult to maintain their virtue in a world where sportsmanship and forbearance count for next to nothing, and "good statistics" and "performance" determine not only how one is paid, but how one is viewed by society and even how one comes to view oneself!

This explains some of the monstrous attitudes that surround and imbue professional sports: their aggressiveness, their obsession with winning, and their total lack of interest in what is "sportsmanlike" behavior, on and off the field, among both spectators and competitors alike! Hence the famous sayings of coach Knute Rockne ("Show me a good loser and I'll show you a loser") and of Red Sanders ("Winning is not everything, it is the only thing") which are nothing if not the creed of modern sports. In reality, such a mentality could hardly be further away from the true, sacred nature and purpose of sport as explained earlier this essay.

One must also mention — for its sheer inanity — the industry of "sports statistics," whereby people ceaselessly calculate and computerize all manner of trivial and almost bizarre information

---

salary and advertisement sponsorships combined)! Now we are the last to say that this or that athlete *in himself* (*or herself*) is not *worthy* of such riches, and obviously whoever pays them does so because they make even more money than that from them. Muhammad Ali, whose personality and boxing skills (marketed and publicized in the 1960s and 1970s by the promoter Don King and the commentator Howard Cossel) largely started the trend of such huge purses being offered to champion athletes, regularly gave half his earnings to charity. He thus seems to us to be, *in himself*, quite worthy of riches. What we do say, however, is that no matter how great the athlete, to earn that much money from making a product and a service out of a sport — especially a sport whose highest meanings are, as we have been saying, misunderstood — cannot but be "undeserved."

comparing the performances of various athletes in various sports, and feed it to the public via newspapers, television, books, computers, radio, news programs, and magazines, encouraging the public to think about them, memorize them, and talk about them. Aside from the fact that one wonders how an adult human being could be truly interested in such desperately meaningless statistics, it has to be said that a frame of mind that can so thoroughly and almost obliviously reduce activities which are by nature so unequivocally qualitative to endless quantifications, is clearly deficient in its scope and its imagination. Indeed, this phenomenon has gone beyond merely being the symptom of a greater moral decay in sports, to the point of being an autonomous affliction in its own right. For there are people in the modern world whose passion and hobby it is to memorize sports and statistics and whose pride and joy it is to engage in mental tussles surrounding such trivia, to the point where some of the most successful television programs in the world are quiz shows where the knowledge of such information is tested! Such people regard it as a positive virtue to know who hit the most "home-runs" in 1987 or who "rushed the most yards" in 1978 and even regard those unconcerned with this kind of information as ignorant or conceited, as if this attitude were itself not the clearest possible proof of true ignorance and conceit as regards the real meaning of sports!

From here it is but one short step to the idolatry of sports champions that has become the hallmark of modern sports spectatorship. Indeed, how else to regard figures whom one has spent countless hours thinking about and whose exploits one has reverently memorized and retold over and over again, especially when, as already mentioned, one has no idea what the true meaning of sport is? Despite the brutal nature of sports and of its champions in their own private lives, few people ever voice the idea that physical prowess is no measure of moral fiber, and that athletes should never *a priori* be regarded as "role models" for anything other than bodily perfection.

No doubt there are other profound reasons why the modern sports hero is regarded as almost sacrosanct, and no doubt these reasons go beyond the financial interests of the sports industry to the fact that the modern world needs heroes,[89] and that athletes are for it "objective" heroes (in the sense that they are easily quantified, this unfortunately being what the modern mentality regards as "objective"), but it nevertheless will not escape anyone that the ideal of bodily perfection is a very mortal one, and for that matter, a very temporal one, and in this sense not very "objective" at all. In previous ages the reason why people did not spend more time on their bodily health and strength was not merely that they had not the luxury or that it was too laborious, but simply because life is short, and the body alone dies. In other words, life is precious, and eternity depends on what we do with it, so it is nothing short

---

89. Films, which are myths of the modern world, are made *ad nauseam* about sports, and although we hope to have occasion elsewhere to explain the reason for this, it will have to suffice herein to name some of the most famous of these to show the extent of the phenomenon: *Chariots of Fire* (athletics); *Heaven can Wait* (football — the film is in fact about a person who delays going to Heaven because he wants to play in the superbowl); *The Longest Yard* (football — the plot is about a convict who becomes willing to stay in jail in order to win a game against the wardens); *Hoosiers* (basketball); *Blue Chips* (basketball); *The Scout* (baseball); *Bull Durham* (baseball — the film starts with the lines: "I believe in the religion of baseball. I've tried all the other religions. . . ."); *A League of Their Own* (woman's baseball); *Field of Dreams* (baseball — which is about souls coming back from Heaven to play that game); *Bad News Bears* (children's baseball); *Rocky I–Rocky V* (boxing); *Raging Bull* (boxing); *Cutting Edge* (ice-skating); *Mighty Ducks* (children's ice-hockey); *Cool Running* (bobsledding); *The Longest Wave* (surfing); *Drop Zone* (parachute jumping); *A River Runs Through It* (fishing); *Tin Cup* (Golf); *Karate Kid* (martial arts, along with hundreds of other such films), and *Dragon* (which is not even about martial arts as such, but about the life of an actor in martial arts films), etc.

of insane to the traditionally minded and intelligent person, to waste it on caring for the only part of oneself that is not immortal, and that makes no difference to God. The body is only a vehicle to get us from one world to another, but the modern mentality, for all its utilitarianism, prizes it above those things — such as the virtues, good deeds left for posterity and love — that really count for us in eternity. The Prophet (ﷺ) said: *When a man dies, all his acts come to an end, but three, recurring charity, knowledge (by which people benefit), or a pious child who prays for him.*[90]

THERE ARE ALSO ills in modern sports which the modern world itself criticizes. The most obvious is the destruction — or hooliganism — that is practiced by supporters of a particular team, club, or country. Parochialism is no doubt the cause of this phenomenon, rather than sports itself, but the two feed off each other in the end. The solution to this problem lies in understanding the difference between a pride that is inclusive and based upon dignity and love of the virtues in one's soul, and a pride that is exclusive and based upon love of oneself wholesale, including one's ego and negative psychic elements. There are two kinds of pride (or "self-love") because there are two different kinds of elements in the soul: good and evil. Only the pride which is impersonally based on love of the good can see the good in others, for the pride based upon love of the ego, cannot love others because it excludes them as they are not "oneself" and because evil simply does not love the good. Fans who mindlessly emphasize their own identity — or "collective self" — without any self-consciousness or restraint have already virtually crossed the line into becoming wild beasts that are willing to crush, by any means possible,

90. Muslim, *Sahih, Kitab al-Wasiyyah*, 14:19.

whatever challenges their sense of self, and thus have already become hooligans even before having damaged anything or anybody else.

The element of destructiveness involved herein is also evidenced in the athletes themselves — though this too is condemned by the modern world — above all in the lengths they are willing to go in order to improve their performances. Drugs, sports psychology, and repeated injury are thus the internal face of the aggression and obsession in sports that externally lead to hooliganism. All too often we hear of a boxer who is "punch-drunk" or steroids causing cancer in a body-builder, despite all the safeguards that sports organizations try to maintain. More underhanded, if not more damaging, than these phenomena is the practice, apparently still widespread, of bribing (or blackmailing) athletes to "fix" matches or games — from boxing to soccer to cricket — in order to win money from bets on the outcome.[91] Most sinister of all, however, is the damage athletes (and those who love them) are willing to inflict on other athletes or competitors, or even animals, whether it be American skaters having their legs broken, Yugoslav tennis stars being stabbed, Columbian soccer players being murdered, or English horses being nobbled, to name just a few actual events of the early 1990s. It is only too obvious that sports should never involve this kind of murderous aggression and the fact that they now do means nothing if not that the modern world, for all its passion for sports, has no idea what their real worth and uses are.

91. Indeed, sports gambling is a huge, international multimillion dollar industry in itself, and of the four major forms of gambling in the world (sports gambling, lottery, casino gambling, and machine gambling) is perhaps the one where the most money changes hands on a regular basis, and needless to say all the traditional criticisms of gambling apply to it as much as to any of the others. Evidently, however, this is an "external" consequence of sports as it is played in the modern world, and has no bearing on sports as such or in themselves, for sports obviously do not necessarily lead to gambling.

All this, then, is to enumerate some of the major ills and abuses not of sport as such, but of sports as practiced in the modern world, and above all of "professional" sports. However, even the modern practice of sports as such has merits in its favor, aside from all the already-mentioned qualities it inherited from its sacred or noble origins. First, modern sports and interest in sport keeps people away from narcotics, for no one who practices sports can in principle (there are of course exceptions) physically afford to be addicted to drugs for this obviously would decimate athletic performance. Moreover, the image surrounding modern sports — for all the subtle hidden ills in them as already mentioned — is ostensibly one of "health consciousness," and obviously the use of narcotics collides head-on with this image. Second, it must be said that modern sports channel violence off the streets of the modern world, or rather that they exhaust some of the violence latent in the people whose nature is inherently explosive, physical, or brutal, or who simply are at an age wherein the strength of their own bodies demands expression or at least an outlet. In other words, modern sports are useful in letting off physical energy within a controlled environment, and, were it not for them, much of this energy might translate itself into social violence. There are, after all, people whose nature inherently predisposes them toward the physical, and it is these people who need sports the most and who can find in them a calling which affords self-fulfillment. Third, despite what has already been mentioned about the parochial affiliations that professional sports encourage on the club, city, and national levels, it must be said that large "sports meets" also generate a positive and culturally constructive kind of ecumenism that breaks down barriers of ignorance and prejudice. Spectators and athletes alike become better informed of other peoples' countries and cultures and learn mutual respect for each other through the demonstration of prowess, skill, and will-power that sports events necessarily require. Moreover, since no single race or country holds an absolute edge over any other in sports contents (unlike in the realms of politics and economics where nuclear power and industrial wealth and technology are quite definitive in their potential consequences, even over collective life and death), sports events inevitably undermine racism and prejudice, as happened precisely in the 1936 Olympic Games where the victories of Black athletes made nonsense of the notion of a "White super-race." Nevertheless, despite these three particular virtues of modern sports, there has still occurred on balance a great impoverishment in sports when compared with their original nature, and the virtues themselves do not make up for all the detrimental elements inherent in the modern "way" of playing sports.

(vi) CONCLUSION:

THIS ESSAY OBVIOUSLY has in no wise exhausted all that can be said about sports, traditional and modern, positive and negative, but we nevertheless trust that it represents a serious and systematic treatment of the subject from a philosophical perspective, and that it can serve as a useful spur to further inquiry on the subject. We have, moreover — in keeping with the nature of philosophy as discussed at the onset — attempted throughout to strike a balance between worldly and metaphysical analysis, a task which was very much in consonance with the nature of the subject itself.

By way of summary, then, let it be said again that sports are sacred or religious in origin, noble in nature, but secularized, abused, and misunderstood in the modern world, and that this is a great shame that could easily be rectified by awareness of their true origin and nature. By way of conclusion let it be said that sports, despite all the ills, corruption, and perversion they now involve, remain in themselves and as such a generally positive phenomenon, useful, edifying, healthy, and commendable.

(vii) APPENDIX A:
THE SYMBOLISM OF CHESS

THERE IS NO game or sport in the world or in history more profound than chess — albeit that there are others perhaps equal to it — for it consists of a symbolism which operates true on a number of different levels. We will endeavor herein to explain a few of the most important of these (in a necessarily simplified manner since it is evidently beyond the scope of these few pages to do so fully), but first a few historical facts about the game need to be established. To start with, then, let it be said that chess originated in India[92] — and therefore is evidently connected with early Hinduism — and that it came to the medieval West through the intermediary of Islam, specifically, through the Persians and the Arabs. Indeed, the very word "checkmate" (German *Schachmatt*) is a combination of the Persian word *shah* meaning "king" and the Arabic word *mat* meaning "dead." Also, the Arabic name for chess *shatranj* itself derives from the Sanskrit word *chaturanga* (which means literally "four-limbed" from the four kinds of auxiliary pieces involved: pawns, knights, bishops, and rooks or castles).

Thus, chess is an ancient game that has been played and contemplated all over the world for many centuries. The ninth-century

---

92. The earliest reference to chess in the surviving Sanskrit literature occurs in about 625. The poet Bana praises the Indian ruler Harsha, who reigned from 606 to 647. Bana describes this king of Kanauj as a prince of peace, noting that in his reign the only wars in the country were among the bees hunting for pollen, the only feet cut off were those in the meter of poetry, and the only armies were those that moved on the sixty-four squares (M. L. Rantala, *A History of Chess: An Essay*, 3).

Arab historian Mas'udi, in his book the *Meadows of Gold*, writes extensively about chess, explaining that, in addition to the form of the board now known to us, there were originally five other kinds of boards in use. He also notes that the rules and meaning of the game have been studied throughout the world long before the ninth century: "The Indians, Greeks, Persians, Byzantines, and other peoples who play chess have described its forms, moves, rules, the explanations that have been given to it, its peculiarities and the setting out of the pieces."[93]

It should also be explained that although chess has been, at one time or another, banned on religious grounds in both Christianity and Islam, in both cases the bans have been for reasons extrinsic to the game itself and have been revoked, ignored, overturned, and deemed wrong by the majority of the religious authorities. Thus in Christianity, although King (and Saint) Louis forbade the game in 1254 — he had in mind the passions aroused by the game when it was accompanied by rolling of the dice (as it was, in the version of it played in those days) — the ban was effectively ended fifty years later by King Alfonso X ("the Wise") who understood the essence of the game better. Similarly, in Islam chess was initially banned by certain early Muslim scholars who based their ban upon a certain *hadith* prohibiting *shatranj* (the Arabic word for chess), but it was later proved that this *hadith* was either apocryphal or referred to a different game by the same name which involved gambling, because chess was not known to the Arabs of Mecca and Medina at the time of the Prophet (ﷺ). And, since Islamic law (*Shariah*) proceeds from the principle of the basic licitness of things unless they are specifically prohibited, the consensus

93. Mas'udi, *The Meadows of Gold*, trans. Lunde and Stone (London; New York: Kegan Paul, 1989), 395–96. See also King Alphonso the Wise of Castile's work *Libros de Acedrex* (1283) for an explanation of one of the most ancient variations of chess, the "game of four seasons."

(*ijma'*) of the Islamic scholars (*'ulema*) is that chess is permissible as long as it does not lead to vices or inhibit the virtues.

Turning now to the symbolism of the game itself, it goes without saying that the first and most obvious level of symbolism of the game refers to war: the pawns represent the soldiers or the light infantry[94]; the knights represent the cavalry; the rooks represent the ancient heavy war chariots; the bishops represent the elephants[95]; the queen represents the "war command" or the "minister"[96]; and the king evidently represents the "supreme commander" or even the "will to fight." As the symbolism and deeper meaning of (holy) war itself have already been mentioned in the text, we will not delve into them again here, and anyway they are implied — if not explicit — in the other levels of symbolism of the game.

The second of these levels of symbolism is cosmological, and, if somewhat less obvious than the first, is no less exact and far more complex:

> The chessboard represents the world. It originated in India, and corresponds to a *mandala*, a simplified representation of the cosmic cycles, which are reproduced in a geometrical scheme on the chessboard. The four centre

94. The logic of why, when a pawn "progresses" to the eighth "rank," it becomes "promoted" to a "minister" or to another piece of the player's choice, will now easily be understood.

95. To this day the Arabic word for "bishop" is "*fil*" meaning literally "elephant": elephants were an essential and effective part of the ancient Hindu armies, and indeed were the only thing that, for example, ever really shook Alexander the Great's army.

96. The figure which today represents the queen was then [in the thirteenth century] the vizier [the "minister"]. In Persian it was known as *fersan*, which became *ferza* in Castilian, *fierce* in Provençal, and finally became *vierge* (virgin) in French [and hence queen in English]. (Titus Burckhardt, *Moorish Culture in Spain*, trans. Alisa Jaffa [New York: McGraw–Hill, 1972], 119)

squares of the chessboard represent the four basic phases of all cycles, ages as well as seasons. The [twelve] squares immediately surrounding them correspond to the orbit of the sun, or the twelve signs of the Zodiac, while the outer of [twenty-eight] squares represent the twenty-eight houses of the moon. The alternatives of black and white is like that of the day and night. The whole square board, which the Indians call *ashtapada*, with its squares of eight by eight, is a "congelation" of the cosmic movements which unfold in time — it is the world. . . . Originally, [chess] was no doubt intended as a cosmic field of battle on which the *devas* and the *asuras*, the angels and the demons, fought one another.[97]

Moreover, each of the eight "major" pieces has a no less exact meaning that corresponds to a cosmological "force" (the pawns — the only "minor" piece in chess — no doubt having a more "earthly" significance):

[There is] a sort of allegory of the heavenly bodies, such as the planets and the twelve signs of the Zodiac, consecrating each piece to a star. . . . It will be noted that the Hindus recognize eight planets: the sun, the moon, the five planets visible to the naked eye, and Rahu, the dark star of the eclipses; each of these "planets" rules one of the eight directions of space.[98]

The third level of symbolism of chess pertains to man himself; more specifically to the soul, its faculties, its possibilities, and its ultimate vocation:

97. Ibid., 118–19.
98. Titus Burckhardt, *Mirror of the Intellect*, trans. William Stoddart, 143.

If the significance of the different chessmen is transposed into the spiritual domain, the king becomes the [subtle] heart, or spirit, and the other pieces the various faculties of the soul. Their movements, moreover, correspond to different ways of realizing the cosmic possibilities represented by the chessboard: there is the axial movement of the "castles" or war chariots, the diagonal movement of the "bishops" or elephants, which follow a single colour, and the complex movement of the knights. The axial movement, which "cuts" through the different "colours," is logical and virile, while the diagonal movement corresponds to an "existential" — and therefore feminine — continuity. The jump of the knights corresponds to intuition.[99]

Evidently, on this level losing one's king means losing access to one's heart, and hence perdition at the end of the "game" (which itself evidently represents earthly life), and checkmating the opponent's king means defeating one's own ego and hence the felicity of winning the "game."

The fourth level of symbolism is in a sense the extension of the previous level: it is the fully "spiritual" symbolism — as opposed to that of the soul (the difference between the two has already been elaborated in section iii of this essay) which only ends, if successful, with attainment unto the Heart and the Spirit — and refers to the stages of the journey "in the Spirit." Indeed, Ibn Arabi wrote a short work — commentated upon and made famous by the Damascene Sheikh Al-Hashemi in this century — entitled *Shataranj Al-Arifun* (*The Chess of the Gnostics*)[100] which describes one hundred different spiritual stations and pitfalls, each of which corresponds to a square

99. Ibid., 147.

100. The chessboard which Ibn Arabi describes is ten alternate black and white squares across by ten alternate black and white squares long, thus making a total of one hundred squares, and not sixty-four as in the current game-board.

on the chessboard, like a great spiritual game of "snakes and ladders" (which obviously itself also contains the same spiritual symbolism), but wherein the moves are consciously determined and not the results of a chance roll of the dice.

Chess also contains a symbolism that refers to the World of the Spirit "as a whole":

> [T]he alternation of black and white corresponds to the two aspects of the *mandala*, which are complementary in principle but opposed in practice: the *mandala* is on the one hand *Purusha-mandala*, that is to say a symbol of the Universal Spirit (*Purusha*) inasmuch as it is an immutable and transcendent synthesis of the cosmos; on the other hand it is a symbol of existence (*Vâstu*) considered as the passive support of divine manifestations. The geometric quality of the symbol expresses the Spirit, while its purely quantitative extension expresses existence. Likewise its ideal immutability is "spirit" and its limiting coagulation is "existence" or *materia*; here it is not *materia prima*, virgin and generous, that is being referred to, but *materia seconda*, "dark" and chaotic, which is the root of existential dualism.[101]

It will not go unnoticed here that there is a certain mirror-play between all the levels of symbolism of chess just mentioned: chess symbolizes at once War (the World Body), the World Soul, man (body, soul, and spirit), and the World Spirit. It is thus "a true symbol"[102] which reflects the whole of manifestation and each of its major dimensions at the same time.

---

101. Burckhardt, *Mirror of the Intellect*, 146.

102. By "true symbol" we obviously mean a "sacred symbol": a symbol that is providentially inherently able to synthesize and reflect, for human meditation, not just the manifested worlds (or essential aspects of them) but the Divine

The last level of symbolism which will be discussed here — doubtless there are others which we have not mentioned — pertains to a person's relationship with his (or her) own destiny. It is one which, perhaps, only more seasoned chess players will fully understand, but one which necessarily concerns everyone, for everyone must confront his or her own destiny, and indeed does so through the moral choices that he or she makes during every conscious instant during life:

> [T]he player learns to curb his passion. The apparently unlimited range of possibilities open to him before each move — provided he has not been driven into a corner — must not lead him to overlook the fact that any false choice will gradually reduce his manoeuvre. This is the law of action, the law of the world, and freedom depends very largely upon knowledge of this law and upon wisdom.[103]

> True wisdom is a more or less perfect identification with the Spirit . . . The Spirit is Truth; through Truth, man is free; outside Truth, he is the slave of fate. That is the teaching of the game of chess. . . .[104]

Archetypes behind them, which gave rise to them in the first place. Every "true symbol" is thus, in a sense, like the ladder in Jacob's dream (Genesis 28:12) for the person able to understand it:

> Each world in the hierarchy of the universe is a reflection of the one above it, and each of its contents reflects, in the higher world, a counterpart which is the immediate source of its existence but which, in its turn, is no more than the reflection of a yet more real counterpart from a yet higher plane of existence. There is thus, for each symbol in the world of matter, a whole series of archetypes one above the other, like the rungs of a ladder, leading up to the Supreme Archetype in the Divine Essence. (M. Lings, *Symbol and Archetype* [Cambridge, Eng.: Quinta Essentia, 1991], 14.)

103. Burckhardt, *Moorish Culture in Spain*, 119.
104. Burckhardt, *Mirror of the Intellect*, 148.

❋

ONE FINAL POINT that bears mentioning about chess in this context, and it is that in addition to all its intrinsic symbolism, chess has come, in our times, to symbolize, extrinsically, the plight of sports in the modern world: nowadays millions, in not tens of millions, of people all over the world play hours and hours of chess, books are written on the subject, contests are organized, and their results are broadcast as national and even international news. Moreover, chess has become a full-time profession for hundreds of players, teachers, and coaches all over the world, and millions of chess computers and programs are constructed and sold which can play and sometimes beat the best human players alive. Indeed, never in history has chess — and perhaps any game — been so popular, but the sole goal in all the current interest in the game is only to win a few rounds and to while away the time. In the whole world there is not more than a handful of people who know the original and real meaning of chess and who therefore can *fully* profit from its spiritual benefits. Thus all the time and energy spent on chess, while pleasant and harmless enough in themselves, nevertheless represent an incalculable waste of potential spiritual benefits. For:

> The *Kshatriya* [the person of the "warrior caste"] who gives himself over to it [chess] does not only find in it a pastime or a means of sublimating his warlike passion and his need for adventure, but also, according to his intellectual capacity, a speculative support, and a Way that leads from action to [spiritual] contemplation.[105]

105. Ibid., 148.

(VIII) APPENDIX B:
CONCENTRATION
IN MODERN SPORTS

MODERN SPORTS, in which athletes are not intentionally focused on any sacred symbols, and which are not consecrated to God as part of a traditional, orthodox religious rite, nevertheless clearly involve intense concentration and dedication on the part of the athletes that practice them, especially since, as already mentioned, they are so fiercely competitive and so much money and prestige hinge upon their results. This concentration — and the preparation for it — takes place, day in, day out, for years on end and more or less throughout an athlete's youth and physical maturity.[106] As such it cannot but have powerful hidden effects on the nature and substance of the athlete's individual soul.

These effects naturally depend upon the athlete's own initial motives and intentions. Thus if the athlete's motives are egotism (which in fact is characterized by wanting everything for oneself, and thus by wanting to win out of sheer selfishness) or anger (some athletes, especially boxers, evoke anger in themselves, which they then release in controlled "spurts," in order to perform more viciously), although this may, on a certain level, help that athlete perform competitively, there occurs *ipso facto* over a long period of time a kind of further "petrifaction" of the psychic elements of

---

106. Most professional athletes nowadays retire at the age of 35, but there are some that go on to 40, and in many sports there are now "Masters' " tournaments for those older still. Serious and competitive athletic training often starts as early as the age of 5!

arrogance and irascibility in that athlete's soul. In other words, as all traditional religions warn,[107] practicing egotistic and baleful actions make one innately more and more egotistic and baleful, because all our actions affect us in an "alchemical" way, and because our actions in the end come to determine who, or what, we are, in our souls. This explains the sheer, untrammeled self-conceit that often characterizes successful modern athletes, and why sometimes the more successful such athletes become in their sport, the more irredeemable they become as people, and this despite all the virtues to be accrued from sports mentioned earlier.

However, not all contemporary professional athletes concentrate for the wrong reasons: some concentrate because of noble, or at least natural, motives, as mentioned earlier. Thus their concentration does not necessarily affect them badly and may even lead to better self-discipline. Moreover, after years of practicing intense concentration many such athletes have reported instances of what they imagine to be a peculiar phenomena typically characterized by "relaxed concentration"[108] and, variously, "focused awareness, complete control of self and environment, and transcendence of self."[109] We quote anecdotal evidence culled from various well-known sportsmen and sportswomen in one of many new books about the subject:

> Every so often a Celtic game would heat so that it would become more than a physical or even mental game, and would be magical. That feeling is difficult to describe and I

107. *Be not deceived; God is not mocked: for whatsoever a man soweth, that shall he also reap.* (Galatians 6:7)

108. Andrew Cooper, *Playing in the Zone: Exploring the Spiritual Dimensions of Sport*, (Boston: Shambhala 1998, *advance uncorrected galleys*) 34.

109. Ibid., 31. Evidently, experiences vary slightly from person to person, but there are basic common factors underlying them all.

certainly never talked about it when I was playing. When it happened I could feel my play rise to a new level. . . . At that special level all sorts of odd things happened. . . . It was almost as if we were playing in slow motion. During those spells I could almost sense how the next play would develop and where the next shot would be taken. . . . My premonitions were consistently correct, and I always felt then that I not only knew all the Celtics by heart but also all the opposing players, and that they all knew me. (Bill Russell, the basketball player, from his autobiography *Second Wind*, written in 1979)[110]

It's a perfect combination of . . . violent action taking place in an atmosphere of total tranquility. . . . It's just having done something that's totally pure and having experienced the perfect emotion, and I'm always sad that I can't communicate that feeling right at the moment its happening. I can only hope people realize what's going on. (Billie Jean King, the tennis player, from her autobiography *Billie Jean*, written in 1974)[111]

It was a type of euphoria; I felt I could run all day without tiring, that I could dribble through any of their team or all of them, that I could almost pass through them physically. I felt I could not be hurt. It was a very strange feeling and one I had not felt before. (Pelé, the soccer player, from his autobiography *My Life and the Beautiful Game*, written in 1977)[112]

110. Ibid., 22-23.
111. Ibid., 23.
112. Ibid., 34

We could go on quoting experiences of such incidents,[113] but it suffices to note that all those who have experienced them note the following two significant details: that they cannot deliberately or consciously induce them,[114] and that self-consciousness, or rather, "self-satisfaction" ends them immediately.[115] Moreover, in modern parlance the experience is now known as "being in *the Zone*," and although "*the Zone* is a cliché for athletes and sports journalists . . . its significance remains as elusive as ever."[116]

So what exactly is *the Zone*, and why and when does it occur? To answer this one need only consider the question: when one drives a car — or just simply walks down the street — fully absorbed in conversation with another person, who is driving the car? Who is directing the walk? Evidently, it is not the soul *per se*, for the soul is then engaged in thinking about the subject that it is discussing. Equally evidently, it is not one of the "subconscious layers" of the soul mentioned earlier, because these are passive. In fact, it is nothing other than what we call in animals "instinct," that is, an "outpost," on the level, of the soul, of the (uncreated) Intellect; a ray originating in the Spirit, but then "filtered" and "refracted." We know it is "filtered" and "refracted" because the proper subject of contemplation of the Intellect is the Divine Nature Itself.[117] We

113. See also Mihalyi Csikszentmihayli's *Flow: The Psychology of Optimal Experience* (New York: Harper and Row, 1990) for the perhaps best known and most thorough modern study about the subject.

114. Cooper, *Playing in the Zone*, 37.

115. Ibid., 118.

116. Ibid., 23.

117. Plato states in his Phaedrus:

Nevertheless the fact is this; for we must have the courage to speak the truth, especially when truth itself is our theme. The region of which I speak is the abode of the reality with which true knowledge is concerned, a reality without colour or shape, intangible but utterly

may thus think of it not as an "intellection" (which may thought of as a flash of Spiritual knowledge, about spiritual things), but rather as an "intuition" (which may be thought of a spiritual flash of knowledge, about ordinary things), only on a lower, more corporeal and hence more animal level. That it is "on a more animal level"[118] is only to be expected since the athletes experiencing *the Zone* are usually focused on entirely physical activities, without any "openings" on sacred symbols or religious rites, and anyway do not usually possess the saintly virtue and purity of soul required for any "higher" kind of intellection.

Why and when does the experience of *the Zone* occur? It occurs because the athlete has at a particular moment concentrated so much and so intensely on a particular activity that he or she has completely forgotten his or her own ego and body — which, as already mentioned, are the primary obstacles to spiritual attainment and are traditionally mortified, in orthodox religions, by *Oratio et Jejunium* — and at that moment the "space of the soul" is

---

real, apprehensible only by the Intellect (*Nous*) which is the pilot of the soul. . . . And in the course of its [the soul's] journey it beholds absolute justice and discipline and knowledge, not the knowledge which is attached to things which come into being, nor the knowledge which varies with the things which we now call real, but the absolute knowledge which corresponds to what is absolutely Real in the fullest sense. (Trans. Walter Hamilton [London: Penguin Books, 1973] 247.

117. It should be pointed an animal's "instinct" and "intelligence" is nothing other than a distant "outpost" of the Universal Intellect (the Macrocosmic equivalent of the human Intellect) under the "veil" of that particular animal's individuality and species. This explains the inner logic and justice of "natural selection": those animals that survive through "natural selection" are those who are "closest" to the Universal Intellect because they are those who are truest to themselves. One might even say, using the contemporary parlance employed above, that those animals in or close to their own *Zones* are the ones that survive the longest through "natural selection."

empty and the Intellect, which is ever-present but usually veiled, is then able to cast into it a "glimmer" of spiritual light.

Does *the Zone* nevertheless have spiritual benefits for the sportsmen and sportswomen who experience it? The answer to this is probably not, for there is no common measure between it and a true Spiritual experience, and because it neither necessarily requires, *a priori*, great virtue nor necessarily gives rise, *a posteriori*, to it (although, conversely, egotism will impede it). However, it might perhaps lead athletes to explore and believe in something other than the physical world, for it is an experience that clearly shows that there are things superior to it. In either case, what it definitely does do is explain moments of astonishing physical performance and impart, to those who witness it, a spectacle of magnificent physical grace and beauty.